Emily E. Ro

I'm Tired, Not Lazy

Recharge Your Life with The Power of Acceptance

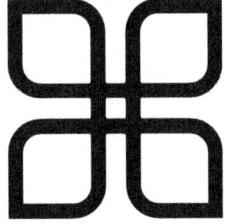

A simple, playful and creative method to rediscover your true self.

Cover design: Justin Greenleaf, Solitonwave.

I'm Tired, Not Lazy: Recharge Your Life with The Power of Acceptance by Emily E. Roberts

Copyright © Emily E. Roberts, 2024
All rights reserved.

Unauthorised reproduction, distribution, or transmission of any part of this publication, including photocopying, recording, or any electronic or mechanical methods, is strictly prohibited without prior written permission from the publisher, except for brief quotations used in reviews and certain noncommercial uses permitted by copyright law.

Disclaimer: This book aims to offer accurate and authoritative information on the covered subject matter. Neither the publisher nor the author is providing psychological or other professional services through its sale. If expert assistance or counselling is required, it is advisable to seek the services of a qualified professional.

Prologue

In this book, I will not provide you with exact advice for practical exercises, but I will guide you through everyday practices with tips and techniques. I aim to guide you on what and how to practice, how to reflect on things, and how to find your own way to reclaim your vitality.

I will cover many aspects that can affect your vitality negatively. I encourage you, after reading the book, to identify those aspects that mostly affect your life and work on them with my guidelines.

Remember, the exercises I provide you with are not meant to be practiced throughout your entire life. After a while, they will become a natural reaction to situations, or they may simply alter your perspective and reactions to different elements in your life.

Throughout the book, I'll repeat certain sentences and concepts. It's not intended to bore you; rather, it's a strategy to embed the essence of the idea deeply within you.

Contents:

Part One: Emily

007......Rise and Shine, or Hit the Snooze Button Like You Mean It?
010......My Morning Yoga Routine: A Dance Class for Insomniacs
013......The Parent Hustle: Where Did I Put the Lunchboxes Again?
016......The Work Hustle: Juggling Deadlines and Coffee Cups
018......The Social Media Struggle: Filters, FOMO, and Finding Balance
021......The Science of Tiredness: More Than Just Monday Blues
025......Letting Go of Perfection: The Liberation of Imperfection
028......Rekindling Passion: Rediscovering the Fire Within
031......Building Better Habits: One Baby Step at a Time
034......Just Let It Go: The Ultimate Liberation

Part Two: Let's Get Serious

037......Introduction: The Liberation in Acceptance
040......Embracing Imperfections: Your Unfiltered Authenticity
045......Letting Go of the Comparison Game: Celebrating Your Unique Journey
048......Acceptance Amidst Chaos: Finding Calm in the Storm
053......Unmasking Vulnerability: The Strength in Being Real
058......Navigating Life's Uncertainties: Embracing the Beauty of the Unknown
062......The Art of Forgiveness: Freeing Yourself from Resentment
065......Mindful Living: Finding Serenity in the Present Moment
069......Letting Go of Control: Surrendering to Life's Flow
074......Acceptance: The Unlikely Superpower
076......Because Even Tired Souls Deserve a Little Sunshine
080......Celebrating Small Wins: Acknowledging Your Progress
084......Acceptance in Relationships: Nurturing Connection Through Understanding
088......Breaking Free from Expectations: Rediscovering Joy on Your Terms
092......Releasing Regret: Embracing the Lessons of the Past
095......The Journey of Self-Compassion: Treating Yourself with Kindness
101......Facing Fear Head-On: Transforming Anxiety into Empowerment

106......MindBodyHarmony: Understanding the Interconnectedness
 of Well-being
110.......Balancing Act: Navigating the Challenges of Work and Life
114.......Resilience in Adversity: Finding Strength in Life's Tests
118.......The Power of Saying "No": Setting Healthy Boundaries
123.......Letting Go of Toxic Influences: Creating Space for Positivity
127.......Embracing Aging: Finding the Wisdom in Growing Older
131.......Self-Care Rituals: Nurturing Your Mind, Body, and Soul
137.......Shifting Focus to the Bright Side of Life
141.......Healing Through Creativity: Expressing Yourself Unapologetically
144.......Reimagining Productivity: Quality Over Quantity
148.......The Role of Laughter: Finding Joy Amidst Life's Challenges
153.......Mindful Eating: Savouring the Pleasures of Nourishment
157.......Accepting Change: The Constant in Life's Equation
162.......Nature as a Therapist: Connecting with the Vitality of the Outdoors
166.......Visualisation Techniques: Envisioning a Vibrant Future
171.......Decluttering for Clarity: Simplifying Life for Inner Peace
174.......Mindful Technology Use: Reclaiming Time for Meaningful Connection
178.......The Power of Rituals: Grounding Yourself in Daily Practices
182.......Acceptance in Grief: Finding Peace in the Midst of Loss
186.......The Liberation in Saying "Yes" to Self-Care
189.......Building a Supportive Community: Connecting with Kindred Spirits
193.......The Journey of Self-Discovery: Accepting and Embracing Change
197.......Celebrating Uniqueness: Loving the Quirks That Make You, You
201.......Cherishing the Gift of Well-being
204.......Rediscovering What Truly Matters
210.......The Power of Silence: Finding Solace in Quiet Reflection
215.......Acceptance in Uncertain Times: Navigating the Unknown with Grace
219.......Respecting Your Energy: Setting Boundaries for Sustainable Vitality
223.......The Joy of Giving: Cultivating a Generous Heart
227.......Letting Go of Perfectionism: Embracing the Beauty in Mistakes
231.......The Beauty of Diversity: Celebrating Differences in Others
235.......Mindful Decision-Making: Choosing Paths Aligned with Your Values
240.......A New Dawn—Reclaiming Your Vitality through Acceptance

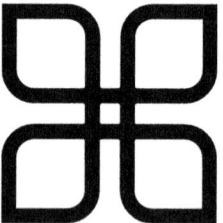

Part one: Emily

Rise and Shine, or Hit the Snooze Button Like You Mean It?

Ah, mornings. The time of day when the birds are chirping, the sun is rising, and I'm wrestling with my mortal enemy: the snooze button. I've come to realise that 'morning persons' are mythical creatures who probably finish a Rubik's Cube before breakfast and then casually run a marathon just for fun. Meanwhile, I'm over here struggling to match my socks.

Let me introduce myself properly. I'm Emily—your not-so-typical protagonist who's just trying to figure out why people willingly wake up before the sun. Like, are they okay? Do they need help? As for me, I treat the snooze button like it's a contestant on a reality show, and I am the ruthless judge deciding its fate.

Now, don't get me wrong. I've tried to be a morning person. I've set countless alarms with optimistic labels like "Early Bird Gets the Worm" and "Rise and Shine, World Dominator." But let me tell you, my inner night owl doesn't take kindly to such propaganda.

The battle begins at 6:00 a.m., or as I like to call it, the middle of the night. My alarm goes off, and my hand instinctively reaches for the snooze button like it's the last piece of chocolate on a deserted island. But here's the kicker: I don't just snooze once. Oh no, I put the 'repeat' in repeat offender. My snooze button is the MVP of my mornings.

As I struggle to pry myself from the warm embrace of my cozy bed, I can't help but envy those people who claim to wake up and conquer the world. Who are these morning wizards? Do they possess some secret potion that I missed out on? Maybe they're born with it, or maybe it's just plain sorcery.

I've heard rumours about these mythical morning beings finishing entire to-do lists before I've even blinked my eyes fully open. They've already meditated, exercised, written a novel, and probably discovered a new species of insect in their backyard. Meanwhile, I'm still negotiating with myself about whether I can skip brushing my hair today.

I'm Now, I know what you're thinking. "Emily, just set one alarm and wake up like a normal person." But where's the fun in that? Life is too short not to hit the snooze button at least three times. It's like a morning tango—a dance of resistance between me and the inevitability of the day.

In my quest for morning person status, I even tried implementing a morning routine. You know, the ones endorsed by successful people who claim to have their lives together. I attempted morning yoga, thinking it would invigorate my soul and turn me into a graceful gazelle leaping into the day.

Reality check: my morning yoga routine looked more like interpretive dance meets a failed attempt at breakdancing. Picture this: limbs flailing, awkward poses, and an occasional stumble. If anyone saw me through the window, they'd probably think a possessed marionette was trying to escape my body.

But here's the twist in my morning saga: despite the chaos, the constant snooze battles, and the failed attempts at morning routines, I've come to a profound realisation. It's not about becoming a morning person or mastering the art of waking up gracefully. It's about accepting that I am not lazy; I am just tired.

Yes, that's right. I'm tired, not lazy. It turns out that my body is not designed to jump out of bed and tackle the day head-on. It's more of a slow, steady roll out of bed with a side order of grumbling. And you know what? That's okay.

In this book, I'm not here to sell you on the idea of waking up at dawn to sing kumbaya with the sunrise. No, I'm here to spill the tea on the real struggles we face—the snooze button battles, the morning mayhem, and the perpetual tiredness that we often mistake for laziness.

So, buckle up, my tired comrades. This is not your typical self-help book. I'm not promising you a magical morning makeover. Instead, I'm inviting you to join me on a journey to reclaim our vitality. It's time to embrace the tiredness, laugh at the chaos, and rediscover the joy in our lives.

Because, my friends, I'm tired, not lazy. And together, we're going to flip the script on exhaustion and make it our superpower. Let the adventure begin!

My Morning Yoga Routine: A Dance Class for Insomniacs

So, I decided to dip my toes into the mystical world of morning yoga. You know, the kind that people swear by to kickstart their day with grace and poise.
My yoga mat probably needed therapy after what I put it through.

I started with the best intentions. Armed with a YouTube tutorial and the determination of someone who's about to conquer Mount Everest (or at least conquer a particularly stubborn jar of pickles), I rolled out my yoga mat.

The instructor on the screen, with their zen-like aura and perfectly executed poses, made it seem like a walk in the park. Little did they know, my park is more like an amusement park on a rollercoaster made of spaghetti.

Let's begin with the first pose: the almighty downward dog. Or, as I like to call it, the "confused cat trying to find its way out of a paper bag." I stuck my butt up in the air like it owed me money and tried to look serene while doing it. But serenity was nowhere to be found.

The yoga instructor's soothing voice guided me through each pose, but my body had other plans. I'd attempt to stretch my arms to the sky, and my limbs would rebel like they were auditioning for a horror movie. The cat, or downward dog, remained confused, probably questioning its life choices.

Next up, sun salutations. Now, I'm not sure why they call it that. Maybe because you're saluting the sun or, more accurately, apologising to it for butchering its namesake poses. Picture me flailing my arms around, attempting to touch my toes without face-planting into the mat. It was less sun salutation and more like an interpretive dance to summon rain.

As I moved from one pose to another, I couldn't help but wonder if the yoga instructor was secretly watching a comedy show. Surely, my attempts at tranquility were more entertaining than a night out at a stand-up gig. I even added my own sound effects—grunts, groans, and the occasional creaking of joints. Yoga meets ASMR, if you will.

The best part? The balance poses. Because who doesn't want to stand on one leg while contemplating the meaning of life? But I couldn't balance a budget, let alone my body on one leg. I wobbled like a newborn giraffe attempting its first steps. I'm pretty sure my neighbours thought I was rearranging furniture or wrestling with an invisible kangaroo.

Midway through the routine, I found myself questioning the life choices that led me to this moment. Was I really so desperate for morning enlightenment that I willingly signed up for this yoga circus? The answer, my friends, was a resounding yes.

But here's the kicker: despite the chaos, the flailing limbs, and the questionable noises emanating from my yoga mat, I felt something. It wasn't the blissful serenity promised by the instructor, but it was a spark of something resembling accomplishment. I mean, I didn't fall flat on my face, so that's a win, right?

As I collapsed onto my yoga mat in a sweaty, panting heap, I realised that maybe yoga wasn't about perfection. Maybe it was about embracing the chaos, finding laughter in the struggle, and not taking ourselves too seriously. After all, life is too short to worry about whether your tree pose looks more like a wilting flower.

So, my fellow yoga warriors, if your downward dog looks like it's trying to escape an invisible box, or your sun salutations summon rain instead of sunshine, fear not. You're not alone. We're all in this together, stumbling our way to fitness glory one confused cat pose at a time.

And as I lay there, contemplating my existence on that yoga mat, I made a pact with myself. I may not become a yoga master, but I will be the master of my own laughter. Because in the grand scheme of life, isn't that the most important pose of all?

The Parent Hustle: Where Did I Put the Lunchboxes Again?

Let's dive headfirst into the chaotic world of parenting—the kind of hustle that makes the stock market look like a Zen garden. Parenting is a full-contact sport, and I'm out here dodging metaphorical tackles like a pro (or at least attempting to).

Meet me on any given weekday morning, and you'll witness a scene straight out of a sitcom. I'm frantically searching for the lunchboxes I swore I packed the night before. They're never where I left them. It's like a lunchbox hide-and-seek game, and those lunchboxes are winning.

As I shuffle through the kitchen, looking under couch cushions and inside the refrigerator (because why not?), I can't help but marvel at the level of ninja stealth my kids' lunchboxes have developed. It's as if they've taken on a life of their own, playing pranks on me and hiding in the most absurd places.

And let's not even talk about school projects. Those innocent-sounding assignments that, in reality, are a test of a parent's ability to improvise and Google the difference between a butterfly and a moth at lightning speed.

It's the night before the big project deadline, and my kid strolls up to me with the classic line, "Mom, I need a poster board and 23 pictures of endangered animals by tomorrow." Panic mode engaged. I find myself raiding the recycling bin for a suitable poster board, googling endangered animals like my life depends on it, and attempting to channel my inner Picasso at 11 p.m.

My poster board looks more like a crime scene collage than an educational masterpiece. But hey, I got it done, and that's what counts, right? Right? Please tell me I'm not the only parent who's produced a subpar project under duress.

Now, let's talk about the morning routine, or as I like to call it, the daily triathlon. Getting the kids dressed, fed, and out the door feels like an Olympic event. It's a race against time, and the clock is not on my side. I've lost this race more times than I care to admit.

There's a moment of triumph when you manage to get the kids into matching socks and shoes, only to realise one of them is wearing yesterday's underwear inside out. The struggle is real, my friends. And don't even get me started on the negotiations over breakfast. It's like a UN peace summit, but with cereal.

As I attempt to wrangle my children into the car, I find myself wondering if parenting classes should be a mandatory prerequisite for reproducing. Because, let's face it, no one warned me about the daily hustle, the lunchbox hide-and-seek, and the last-minute school projects that come with this parenting gig.

But here's the twist: amid the chaos, the sleep-deprived negotiations, and the frantic search for missing shoes, there's laughter. Yes, you heard me right—laughter. Because if you can't find humour in the midst of the parent hustle, you might just end up in a straightjacket.

I've learned to appreciate the absurdity of it all. The moments when my kid insists on wearing a superhero cape to school or when I accidentally pack a lunchbox full of snacks and forget the actual lunch.

And let's not forget the joy of receiving artwork that looks more like abstract expressionism than a recognisable drawing. "Is this a dinosaur or a potato with legs?" I find myself asking, trying to decipher the creative genius of a six-year-old.

But in the grand scheme of things, these are the moments that make the parent hustle worth it. The messy, chaotic, unpredictable moments that become the stories you tell at family gatherings or, in my case, write about in a book.

So, as you navigate the labyrinth of lost lunchboxes and navigate the minefield of school projects, remember this: you're not alone. We are collectively involved in this situation, dodging obstacles, laughing at the absurdity, and occasionally wondering if we've lost our minds.

And as I sit here, surrounded by mismatched socks, half-eaten granola bars, and the remnants of a failed attempt at a Pinterest-worthy school project, I wouldn't have it any other way. Because, my friends, the parent hustle is a wild ride, and I'm here for every hilarious, chaotic moment of it.

And in the midst of the madness, I've come to accept that perfection is overrated.

The Work Hustle: Juggling Deadlines and Coffee Cups

Welcome to the turbulent circus that is my professional life. I call it a circus because there's always an element of danger, and occasionally, someone might get hit by a metaphorical pie in the face. If only those pies were made of caffeine, I'd be invincible.

I'm standing in the centre ring, surrounded by deadlines flying at me like flaming torches. It's a real-life juggling act, and I'm not even sure if I'm holding the right end of the torches. Sometimes they feel more like medieval weaponry than project timelines.

My alarm clock is my call to the big top, and let me tell you, the snooze button is my arch-nemesis. I hit it with the desperation of a cat trying to bat away a laser pointer dot. But the circus doesn't wait for anyone, not even the Snooze Button Warrior. The show must go on, and I drag myself out of bed, still half-asleep, hair resembling a bird's nest, ready to face the corporate lions.

First things first, caffeine. Coffee is my spirit animal, my lifeline, my co-worker of the year. I have a mug that's so big; I can practically swim in it. I call it my Sea of Sanity. Without it, I'm just a ship lost at sea, and my deadlines are the sharks circling.

The office coffee machine is a treacherous place. It's like playing Russian roulette with caffeine addiction. Will it be the dark roast that gives you superhero energy, or the decaf that mocks your existence? You never know. I once accidentally drank decaf, and my day felt like an episode of the Twilight Zone. My colleagues would talk to me, but their words sounded like gibberish. I was in a caffeine-less alternate reality.

Once I've navigated the coffee conundrum, it's time for the true spectacle—the work hustle. I dive into my emails, and it's like stepping into a minefield. Boom! Urgent project update. Boom! Meeting rescheduled. Boom! Coffee machine on the fritz again. The horror!

Deadlines are like sneaky little shadow warriors, always lurking in the shadows. You think you've got everything under control, and then BAM! A shadow warrior deadline throws a smoke bomb, and suddenly, your project is due tomorrow.

But here's the trick – you've got to dance with the deadlines. I've perfected the art of the last-minute hustle, where I channel my inner superhero and swoop in to save the day. It's a risky move, but hey, risks are what make life thrilling, right?

Now, let's talk about office politics. It's a jungle out there, and I'm not just referring to the break-room fridge. Navigating the delicate ecosystem of coworkers is an art form. There are the friendly pandas who just want to share their bamboo shoots (read: office gossip), the territorial lions guarding their turf, and the elusive chameleons who blend in with every team.

But amidst the chaos, there's a silver lining – the office nap. Oh yes, you heard me right. I have discovered the secret sanctuary of rejuvenation – the nap pod. It's like a cocoon of tranquility, a brief escape from the circus. I sneak in there, set an alarm, and drift into a power nap. It's the ultimate rebellion against the 9-to-5 grind.

Now, I'm not saying you should nap at your desk; that's a surefire way to become the office meme. But find a quiet corner, a cozy chair, or if you're lucky, a nap pod, and embrace the rejuvenating power of a well-timed siesta. It's the secret weapon of productivity, and trust me, your colleagues will wonder how you manage to be so zen amidst the chaos.

As I juggle deadlines and coffee cups, I've learned that the key to surviving the work hustle is not taking yourself too seriously. Dance with the deadlines, sip your Sea of Sanity, and when the circus gets overwhelming, sneak away for a clandestine nap. Embrace the chaos, my friend, because life is too short to be a serious juggler. It's time to join the circus and make it your own hilarious spectacle.

The Social Media Struggle: Filters, FOMO, and Finding Balance

Step right into my digital spectacle, where the conductors of the show are none other than the Instagram filters, FOMO is the resident clown, and finding balance is the ultimate tightrope act. We're diving into the world of social media, where reality is a distant cousin, and perfection is just a swipe away.

Let's talk filters, shall we? Those magical little creatures that turn Monday morning bedhead into Saturday night glam. I've tried them all—Glamour, Vintage, Valencia, you name it. But here's the kicker: filters are like that friend who insists on telling you they're fine when you know they've had a rough day. They're hiding the imperfections, smoothing out the wrinkles, and adding a touch of magic that makes you question if your life is a low-budget indie film.

I fell into the filter rabbit hole like Alice after one too many cups of tea. There I was, scrolling through the options, contemplating whether to be a sepia-toned goddess or a black-and-white mysterious stranger. I went with the sepia, because nothing says mystery like a vintage filter, right?

But let's get real. Filters are the ultimate optical illusion. They turn your living room into a tropical paradise, your instant noodles into a Michelin-starred meal, and your quarantine outfit into a runway ensemble. It's like having a personal Photoshop assistant who follows you around, making sure every moment is Instagram-worthy. But, truth be told, life is better without perfect filters.

And then there's FOMO—the Fear of Missing Out, the perpetual party crasher of the digital age. FOMO is like that annoying friend who never stops texting you, telling you about the epic party you're missing while you're in your pyjamas, binge-watching Netflix. It's the modern-day version of keeping up with the Joneses, but now the Joneses are on a beach in Bali, and you're stuck in traffic on your way to work.

We've all been there, right? Scrolling through social media, seeing friends living their best lives, while you're contemplating if ordering pizza counts as cooking. FOMO is the master of illusion, making you believe everyone else has it figured out while you're still searching for matching socks. But here's the plot twist:

nobody has it all figured out. We're all just winging it, and those perfect Instagram photos are often just carefully curated moments in a sea of chaos.

So, how do we find balance in this digital circus? Well, first, we need to accept that life is messy, unfiltered, and sometimes downright ridiculous. It's okay if your living room looks like a tornado hit it, and your dinner is more microwave than Michelin. Embrace the imperfections, my friends, because that's where the real magic happens.

Next up, let's talk about the scrolling marathon. We've all experienced that situation before, lost in the abyss of social media, swiping up like our life depends on it. It's a digital black hole that can suck you in, leaving you dazed and confused, wondering where the last hour went. But fear not, because I've discovered the antidote: the social media detox.

I'm not saying you have to delete all your apps and go live in a cave, although that does sound tempting sometimes. No, a social media detox is like hitting the reset button on your digital brain. Take a break, go for a walk, read a book, or simply stare at a wall and contemplate the meaning of life. Trust me; your sanity will thank you.

And now, let's talk about authenticity, the unsung hero in the world of social media. It's easy to get lost in the sea of influencers, celebrities, and people who seem to have it all together. But the real power lies in being true to yourself. Post the messy hair, the failed cooking attempts, and the days when you'd rather be in bed than conquering the world. Authenticity is your secret weapon against the digital facade.

Life is not a highlight reel, my friends. It's a messy, beautiful, unfiltered journey, and the sooner we embrace it, the happier we'll be. So, let's ditch the perfect filters, laugh in the face of FOMO, and find the balance that makes the digital circus a place of joy, not comparison.

The Science of Tiredness: More Than Just Monday Blues

Today, we're putting on our lab coats, grabbing a magnifying glass, and diving into the science of tiredness. Strap in, because it's about to get geeky in here, and I promise not to use words that sound like spells from a Hogwarts textbook.

So, let's talk about circadian rhythm. Sounds fancy, right? Like something you'd discuss in a dark room with beakers and mysterious potions. But no, it's not as Hogwarts-y as it sounds. Circadian rhythm is basically your body's internal clock, the puppet master behind your sleep-wake cycle. It's like having a tiny DJ in your brain, playing the tracks of alertness and drowsiness. And guess what? This DJ doesn't care if it's Monday or Friday; it just follows its rhythm.

Now, here's where it gets interesting. Our bodies love routine, and this DJ thrives on it. It's like telling your brain, "Hey, DJ, we're hitting the hay at 11 PM every night, understand?" But life, being the unpredictable party crasher it is, throws in late-night emails, Netflix binges, and existential crises. Suddenly, the DJ is spinning tracks at 2 AM, and your circadian rhythm is doing the Macarena in confusion.

I used to blame Mondays for my perpetual tiredness. Monday Blues, they call it. But the truth is, our circadian rhythm doesn't give a damn about weekdays. It's just doing its thing, day in and day out. So, if you're feeling like a zombie on a Wednesday, blame the DJ, not the calendar.

Mitochondria. No, it's not a new workout craze or a mystical energy crystal. Mitochondria are the powerhouse of your cells, the Energiser bunnies keeping you going. These tiny fellas churn out ATP, the energy currency of your body. Picture them as the factory workers in a chocolate factory, but instead of chocolates, they're cranking out energy bars for your cells.

However, here's the twist – mitochondria can get tired too. They're like the interns working overtime in the chocolate factory. Give them too much work, and they'll start protesting. Suddenly, your energy production slows down, and you're left wondering why a flight of stairs feels like Mount Everest.

Imagine this: you're burning the midnight oil, working on that project, and your mitochondria are pulling double shifts. They're sending you signals like, "Hey, Emily, we need a break," but you're too busy chugging coffee and channeling your inner superhero. It's a classic case of miscommunication. Your mitochondria are sending SOS signals, and you're responding with, "Just five more minutes!"

And let's not forget about the stress hormone cortisol. It's like that unwanted party crasher who barges in when you least expect it. Cortisol is supposed to help you deal with stress, but too much of it is like having a hyperactive toddler on a sugar rush. It messes with your sleep, throws off your circadian rhythm, and before you know it, you're stuck in a cycle of fatigue and cortisol-induced chaos.

Now, I won't bore you with more science terms, but the point is, fatigue is a complex symphony of factors. It's not just about burning the midnight oil or blaming Mondays. It's about understanding the dance between your circadian rhythm, mitochondria, and the hormonal amusement ride happening inside you.

But fear not, my tired comrades, because I've got the cheat codes to decode this fatigue puzzle. First and foremost, let's be kind to our circadian rhythm. Give it a schedule, a routine, and let that DJ play its tracks without unexpected remixes.

Next, show some love to your mitochondria. They may be tiny, but they're the unsung heroes of your energy game. Feed them well with a balanced diet, exercise, and let them take breaks. Think of it as a chocolate factory retreat for your hardworking interns.

And when cortisol comes knocking, do a little meditation, take a walk, or scream into a pillow if that's your thing. Just don't let it run wild in your system. It's all about finding the balance, like a circus performer on a tightrope, gracefully navigating the complexities of your body.

So, my tired warriors, it's time to stop blaming Mondays and start understanding the science behind your fatigue. Embrace your circadian rhythm, pamper your mitochondria, and show cortisol who's boss. Because the real magic happens when you decode the science and dance to the rhythm of your own energy symphony.

And remember, it's not just about surviving Mondays; it's about conquering every day with the knowledge that your body is a complex, resilient masterpiece.

And there you have it, the lowdown on the science behind our perpetual fatigue. Now armed with knowledge about circadian rhythms, mitochondria, and the unruly cortisol, you're ready to navigate the labyrinth of tiredness like a seasoned pro.

But don't worry! Practical advice is just around the corner. In the upcoming chapters, we'll dive into actionable tips to befriend your circadian rhythm, pamper your hardworking mitochondria, and give cortisol the boot. We'll decode the fatigue puzzle together, sprinkled with a dash of "just let it go."

So, stay tuned for the practical wisdom that will transform fatigue into a distant memory. Through it all, remember the power of acceptance. Together, we'll embrace the circus, sip from our Sea of Sanity, and embark on the journey ahead – because understanding and accepting our bodies is the key to unlocking a life filled with newfound energy.

Letting Go of Perfection: The Liberation of Imperfection

Let's start with the elephant in the room: perfection. It's like that unattainable crush we all had in high school – alluring from a distance, but once you get close, you realise it's just a mirage. Perfection is the illusion that taunts us, makes us feel like we're perpetually falling short. Well, guess what? Perfection is overrated, and striving for it is like chasing a rainbow that keeps moving away.

I used to be the poster child for perfectionism. Everything had to be flawless – my work, my appearance, my life. It was exhausting, and I was one tired perfectionist. But then I had an epiphany – perfect is boring. Imperfection, now that's where the party's at.

Letting go of perfection is like shedding a heavy coat you've been lugging around. Suddenly, you're free to dance, make mistakes, and embrace the beautifully messy chaos of life. It's liberating, my friends, and it's time to liberate yourselves from the perfection prison.

Let me share a little secret with you. The messiness of life is where the real magic happens. It's in the spilled coffee, the tangled hair, and the unfiltered laughter that escapes when you least expect it. Perfection is a stiff, formal party where everyone's afraid to break a glass. Imperfection is the wild house party where you dance on tables and sing karaoke at 2 AM. Which one sounds more fun to you?

Now, I get it; letting go of perfection is easier said than done. Society bombards us with images of flawless lives, flawless bodies, flawless everything. But guess what? Those flawless lives are about as real as a unicorn riding a unicycle. We're all navigating this messy journey called life, and the sooner we embrace the chaos, the happier we'll be.

Let's talk about expectations, shall we? We set these ridiculously high standards for ourselves, thinking that perfection will bring us happiness. But the truth is, it's a never-ending game. You hit one milestone, and suddenly there's another mountain to climb. It's like playing a game of whack-a-mole with your own expectations.

I used to believe that if I reached a certain level of perfection, I'd finally be content. But every time I got close, the bar would move higher. It's like trying to win a limbo competition, but the limbo stick keeps getting lower. So, I decided to ditch the limbo stick and embrace the messy, imperfect limbo dance of life.

Letting go of perfection is not giving up; it's gaining freedom. It's about saying, "You know what? I'm not perfect, and that's perfectly okay." It's liberating yourself from the shackles of unrealistic standards and giving yourself the permission to be gloriously, unapologetically imperfect.

Let's delve into the topic of the fear of judgment. We're so terrified of being judged that we put on this facade of perfection, hoping nobody will see through the cracks. But here's the truth – people relate to imperfection. Nobody wants to be friends with a robot; they want to be friends with someone who spills their coffee and laughs it off.

Think about your favourite people – the ones you genuinely connect with. Are they the ones with flawless lives and perfect exteriors, or are they the ones who embrace their quirks, flaws, and the beautiful messiness that makes them uniquely human? Imperfection is the glue that bonds us, my friends, and it's time to let go of the fear of judgment and embrace the real you.

So, how do we do it? How do we liberate ourselves from the chains of perfectionism? Well, it starts with self-compassion. Treat yourself like you would treat your best friend. When you make a mistake, instead of beating yourself up, give yourself a hug and say, "Hey, we're all human, and imperfection is what makes us interesting."

Next up, let's talk about failure. Oh, the F-word that sends shivers down our spines. But here's the reality check – failure is not the opposite of success; it's a part of it. The most successful people in the world have a long list of failures behind them. So, embrace failure like a long-lost friend, because it's the stepping stone to growth and resilience.

And finally, let's redefine success. It's not about achieving perfection; it's about progress. Life is not a checklist; it's a journey. Celebrate the small wins, learn from the losses, and remember that perfection is an illusion, but progress is real.

Together, we'll liberate ourselves from the pressure to be perfect and discover the joy that comes with being beautifully, authentically imperfect.

Rekindling Passion: Rediscovering the Fire Within

Remember those personal dreams? The ones you had before life decided to throw responsibilities and adulting in your face like a surprise pie? Well, my friends, it's time to dust off those dreams, peel off the layers of doubt, and rekindle the fire within. Trust me; it's like hitting the reset button on your soul.

Let me set the scene for you. There I was, buried under the avalanche of everyday life – work, family, the never-ending laundry saga – you know the drill. But in the midst of the chaos, I heard a faint whisper. A whisper that said, "Hey, remember me? Your dreams? I'm still here, waiting for you to pick me up and run with me."

So, I embarked on this journey of rediscovering my passion. Step one: acknowledging that I had buried my dreams under the debris of adulting. Step two: excavating those dreams like an archeologist on a mission. And step three: reigniting the flames of passion, even if it meant burning a few outdated beliefs in the process.

Rediscovering your passion is not a smooth, paved highway. It's more like a bumpy, winding road with unexpected potholes and detours. You'll question your GPS, curse at the road signs, but damn, it's one hell of a ride.

First stop on this passion quest: self-reflection. I had to ask myself the hard questions. What truly makes my heart race? What brings that spark to my eyes? And most importantly, what would I do if I weren't afraid to fail? Let me tell you, these questions are like throwing open the windows of a stuffy room. Suddenly, fresh air rushes in, and you start seeing possibilities you never knew existed.

Now, let's talk about setbacks. Oh, the delightful curveballs life likes to throw our way. Just when I thought I was gaining momentum on my passion journey, bam! Life hit me with a curveball, and I stumbled. But here's the thing about setbacks – they're not roadblocks; they're detours. It's like taking a scenic route that shows you unexpected beauty along the way.

I faced rejection, failure, and moments when I questioned if pursuing my passion was just a whimsical fantasy. But here's the truth: setbacks are the universe's way of testing your commitment. Do you really want this? How bad are you willing to fight for it? And let me tell you, I fought. I fought like a mama bear protecting her cubs because passion is worth fighting for.

Let's discuss the 'F' word – fear. Oh, fear, the saboteur of dreams. I was terrified. Terrified of failing, of judgment, of the unknown. But fear is not the enemy; it's a companion on the journey. It's the sidekick that whispers, "Hey, this is important to you. Let's face it together." So, I faced my fears head-on, armed with the knowledge that passion is a good look on everyone.

Rekindling passion is not about avoiding fear; it's about dancing with it. It's about turning fear into the rhythm that propels you forward, the adrenaline that fuels your pursuit. And let me tell you, when you face your fears, you emerge stronger, wiser, and with a newfound swagger that says, "I'm here, and I'm not backing down."

Time. The elusive, ever-ticking clock that likes to remind us that we're not getting any younger. I used to think, "Oh, I'll pursue my passion when the stars align, and the universe gives me a permission slip." The universe doesn't hand out permission slips. You have to grab your passion by the horns and ride it like a wild bull.

Rekindling passion is not about waiting for the perfect moment; it's about creating the perfect moment. It's about taking those small, intentional steps every day, even when life is throwing its chaotic symphony at you. Trust me; the universe loves a go-getter.

So, how do you keep the flames of passion burning bright amidst the chaos of life? Well, it starts with prioritising. Carve out time for your passion, even if it's just fifteen minutes a day. You wouldn't skip your morning coffee, right? Treat your passion with the same devotion.

Next, surround yourself with like-minded fire starters. Join communities, attend events, and connect with people who share your passion. Passion is contagious, my friends, and being in the company of fellow dream chasers fuels your own fire.

And remember, it's okay to pivot. Your passion may evolve, take unexpected turns, and that's the beauty of it. It's not a rigid destination; it's a dynamic journey. Be flexible, adapt, and let your passion flow like water, finding its way around obstacles.

Building Better Habits: One Baby Step at a Time

Building habits can be as challenging as learning to ride a bike for the first time. The initial wobbling and uncertainty make it a journey filled with both frustration and the promise of eventual mastery.. It's confusing, frustrating, and you might accidentally end up with mismatched colours. But fear not, my friends, because we're about to break it down into bite-sized, manageable pieces. No blindfold required.

First things first, let's talk about the myth of overnight transformation. We live in a world where the idea of instant change is dangled in front of us like a shiny carrot. Want to get fit? Just do a 30-day challenge. Want to become a morning person? Just wake up at 5 AM tomorrow. Spoiler alert: it's a trap.

Overnight transformations are like crash diets. Sure, you might see quick results, but they're not sustainable, and you'll end up binging on bad habits faster than you can say kale smoothie. Building better habits is a marathon, not a sprint. It's about creating a lifestyle that sticks, and that, my friends, requires patience, consistency, and a dash of humour.

Alright, let's discuss the power of baby steps. Imagine trying to climb Mount Everest in one giant leap. Sounds absurd, right? Building better habits is no different. It's about taking small, manageable steps that you can sustain, like climbing a staircase instead of attempting the Everest leap.

I used to think that if I wasn't making drastic changes, I wasn't making progress. I was wrong. Baby steps are like the unsung heroes of habit-building. They're small, seemingly insignificant, but they add up, and before you know it, you're standing on the summit of your own personal Everest.

So, how do we take these baby steps without feeling like we're tiptoeing through a minefield of potential failures? Well, it starts with setting realistic goals. Instead of aiming for the moon, aim for the nearest rooftop. Want to start exercising? Start with a ten-minute walk. Want to eat healthier? Add one serving of veggies to your meals. The key is to set goals that are so ridiculously doable, you can't say no.

Consistency. Consistency is like the glue that holds the baby steps together. It's not about doing something once and expecting life-altering changes. It's about showing up, even on the days when you'd rather cozy up with a bag of chips and call it a night. Consistency is the secret sauce that transforms baby steps into habit gold.

And now, the game-changer: create triggers. Triggers are like little reminders that nudge you in the right direction. Want to build a reading habit? Place a book next to your coffee maker. Want to exercise in the morning? Sleep in your workout gear. Triggers make the baby steps automatic, like brushing your teeth or checking your phone for the twentieth time.

But let's talk about the inevitable setbacks, shall we? Setbacks are not the end of the world; they're just plot twists in the story of habit-building. Life happens, and there will be days when your baby steps turn into baby stumbles. The key is not to throw in the towel and declare defeat. It's about dusting yourself off, reminding yourself that you're human, and continuing the journey.

I faced setbacks, oh boy, did I face setbacks. Missed workouts, late-night Netflix binges, and days when my to-do list resembled a Jackson Pollock painting. But instead of spiralling into guilt and self-loathing, I embraced the setbacks as opportunities to reassess, adjust, and keep going.

Accountability partners are like the Batman to your Robin, the Thelma to your Louise. They're there to cheer you on, kick your butt when needed, and share the journey. It could be a friend, a family member, or even an app that sends you annoying reminders. Accountability partners make the baby steps a team effort, and suddenly, the journey becomes a lot less lonely.

And here's a game-changer – celebrate the wins, no matter how small. Finished a workout? Treat yourself to a bubble bath. Ate a serving of veggies? Give yourself a high-five. The journey of building better habits is a series of victories, and each one deserves its moment in the spotlight.

Just Let It Go: The Ultimate Liberation

We're diving into the holy grail of wisdom—letting go. Picture this as a giant balloon release for your soul, where you untether yourself from the unnecessary, the unrealistic, and the downright exhausting. Letting go is the key to unlocking a life that's lighter, brighter, and more energised. Just let it go, and let the laughter in.

Let's start with the unnecessary weight we carry—the baggage that's not serving us. We accumulate this baggage like souvenir magnets on a never-ending vacation. The guilt, the regrets, the "what-ifs" that weigh us down like anchors in a stormy sea. But guess what? You're not a cargo ship; you're a sleek, badass yacht ready to navigate the open waters.

It's time to Marie Kondo your emotional baggage. Does it spark joy? If not, toss it overboard. Guilt about that dessert you had last night? Let it go. Regret about that cringe-worthy moment from five years ago? Adios. The unnecessary weight is not a status symbol; it's a burden, and it's time to sail into the sunset with a lighter load.

Let's discuss the topic of unrealistic expectations—the silent dream killers that lurk in the shadows. We set these expectations like traps, hoping they'll catch success and happiness. Expectations are like the mousetrap that snaps on your finger instead. It's time to release ourselves from the grip of these expectation traps.

I used to expect myself to be this perfect, multitasking superhero. I'm not Wonder Woman; I'm more like Wonder-How-Did-I-End-

Up-in-This-Mess Woman. But here's the liberating truth—perfection is an illusion, and expectations are the architects of that illusion. Let them go, my friends, and embrace the beautifully messy reality of your existence.

Self-imposed pressures—the unnecessary deadlines, the arbitrary timelines that turn life into a race against an invisible clock. I used to feel this constant pressure to have it all figured out by a certain age. Life is not a math problem with a single correct solution.

It's time to dismantle the ticking time bomb of self-imposed pressures. Life doesn't come with a roadmap, and that's the beauty of it. The twists, the turns, the detours—they're all part of the adventure. So, let go of the need to have it all mapped out. Embrace the uncertainty, and trust that the journey is leading you exactly where you need to be.

Now, the ultimate wisdom: just let it go. It's not just a catchy phrase; it's a mantra for living. Let go of the things that no longer serve you, the expectations that stifle you, and the pressures that weigh you down. Liberating yourself is not a one-time event; it's a daily practice of shedding the unnecessary layers.

Just imagine you're in a hot air balloon, and each let-it-go moment is a sandbag dropping away. Guilt—drop. Expectations—drop. Pressures—drop. The higher you go, the lighter you become. The clearer the view, the more you can see the beauty of life unfolding below. So, let go, my friends, and soar to new heights.

Now, you might be thinking, "Emily, this sounds great, but how do I actually let it go?" Well, I've got the keys to the letting-go kingdom.

First, practice self-compassion. Treat yourself like you would treat your best friend. When that inner critic starts whispering, drown it out with self-love. You're doing the best you can, and that's more than enough.

Next, adopt a gratitude mindset. Instead of focusing on what's lacking, shift your perspective to what you have. Gratitude is the antidote to the poison of scarcity. It's like turning on the lights in a dark room; suddenly, everything becomes clearer, and you realise there's more than enough.

And the magic ingredient: laughter. Laughter is the ultimate elixir for letting go. It's the release of tension, the breaking of chains, and the affirmation that life is meant to be enjoyed, not endured. So, surround yourself with things that make you laugh – comedy shows, funny friends, and maybe even a mirror to admire your own ridiculous expressions.

The beauty of letting go is that it creates space for laughter, joy, and the unexpected. Life becomes a playground, not a battlefield. You stop wrestling with the universe and start dancing with it. Letting go is not a surrender; it's a liberation.

And now, let's get serious—seriously ready for a life that doesn't require a nap after breakfast. Letting go is not just a chapter ending; it's the beginning of a liberating journey ahead.

Part Two: Let's Get Serious

Introduction: The Liberation in Acceptance

Hey there tired souls, weary wanderers, and anyone who's ever felt like a sloth in a world full of energiser bunnies. Welcome to my little corner of the universe, where we're about to embark on a journey from the land of perpetual fatigue to the promised land of renewed vitality. Grab a comfy chair (preferably one that doesn't judge you for taking a nap), and let's dive into the liberating world of acceptance.

Picture this: You're dragging yourself out of bed, eyelids heavy enough to rival the weight of a thousand elephants. The coffee maker becomes your morning deity, and you're convinced that if someone were to offer you a caffeine IV drip, you'd sign up in a heartbeat. Life feels like a never-ending loop of exhaustion, and the word 'lazy' starts sticking to you like an unwanted nickname.

That's where I found myself, stuck in the quicksand of perpetual tiredness, trying to convince myself that maybe, just maybe, I was a lazy blob. I wasn't. And chances are, if you're reading this, you aren't either.

So, here's the deal: In this chapter, we're going to talk about the game-changer, the magic word that turned my world around – acceptance. It's not just about acknowledging that you're tired; it's about embracing it, throwing a little party for your worn-out self, and realising that it's okay not to have it all together all the time.

Let's rewind a bit. There I was, living my life in what felt like slow motion, as if someone had hit the 'snooze' button on my energy levels. Mornings were a struggle, afternoons were a blur, and by the time evening rolled around, I was practically a walking zombie.

In my quest to decode this exhaustion mystery, I stumbled upon a revelation – I wasn't lazy. It wasn't a lack of ambition or a secret desire to spend my days binge-watching sitcoms (although, let's be real, that can be tempting). It was good old-fashioned tiredness, the kind that creeps into your bones and refuses to budge.

Now, let's talk about acceptance. It's not a flashy concept, and it won't solve all your problems overnight, but trust me, it's the secret sauce to transforming exhaustion into empowerment. Acceptance is like that wise friend who looks at you and says, "Hey, it's okay not to be okay."

Acceptance isn't about waving a white flag and surrendering to a life of perpetual fatigue. No, no, my friend. It's about understanding that fatigue is a part of the human experience. It's about recognising that you're not alone in this battle, and it's perfectly fine to cut yourself some slack.

Imagine acceptance as a liberating dance – a waltz with your limitations and a tango with your tiredness. It's about putting on your favourite comfy socks, cranking up the music, and embracing the rhythm of your own journey.

Acceptance doesn't mean giving up; it means letting go of the guilt and shame that often accompany exhaustion. It's about peeling off the layers of societal expectations and letting your tired, beautiful self shine through.

Journal Prompts:

Now it's time for some soul-searching. Get yourself a notebook, or open a new document on your digital device of choice, and let's dive into these journal prompts:

1. What does tiredness mean to me?
Explore your personal relationship with fatigue. Is it a sign of weakness, or can it be a source of strength?

2. List three moments when you felt the weight of exhaustion.
Reflect on specific instances when tiredness took centre stage. What emotions surfaced, and how did you react?

3. If tiredness had a soundtrack, what songs would be on it?
Get creative! Assign a playlist to your fatigue. Is it a slow ballad or an upbeat anthem? What does your tiredness groove to?

4. How would I describe acceptance in my own words?
Define acceptance in a way that resonates with you. What does it look like in your life?

Remember, this is your journey, and there's no rush. Take your time, embrace the tired moments, and get ready for the adventure that lies ahead.

Embracing Imperfections: Your Unfiltered Authenticity

Now, let's progress to the next stage of our expedition: embracing imperfections with the finesse of a seasoned improviser. Brace yourself—it might not always be a seamless performance, but the liberation that comes with it is worth the endeavour.

In the realm of social media, the illusion of perfect lives often leaves us marvelling at flawless photos, impeccable smiles, and seemingly charmed existences. However, it's time to unveil the truth: those flawless lives are as real as unicorns. In this chapter, we're dismantling the myth of perfection and shining a spotlight on the beauty of imperfections, because your authentic, messy, and gloriously imperfect self deserves applause.

Allow me to recount a moment from my own life, a narrative that encapsulates the comedy of errors that characterises my existence. — I'm sprinting late for a meeting, my hair in a messy bun that defies gravity, a coffee stain embellishing my shirt, and mismatched socks subtly protesting my fashion sense. To add a touch of slapstick, I trip over an invisible pebble during my entrance.

In that moment, acceptance became my superhero cape. Rather than succumbing to embarrassment, I embraced the pandemonium. I walked into that meeting with a coffee-stained shirt, unruly hair, and a newfound sense of liberation. It felt like shedding the weight of pretending to have it all together.

Now, it's your turn to revel in imperfections with a dash of humour. Here's a practical exercise to unleash the unfiltered authenticity within you:

1. The Imperfection Inventory:
Open your journal and list three aspects of yourself that you consider imperfect. These could be physical quirks, habitual tendencies, or even endearing yet awkward idiosyncrasies. Embrace these imperfections as the unique brushstrokes on the canvas of your life.

2. The Comedy Routine:
Transform those imperfections into a comedy routine. Envision yourself as a stand-up comedian, crafting a humorous script that highlights the charm in your quirks. Feel free to exaggerate gestures and throw in a few goofy sound effects for good measure.

3. The Mirror Pep Talk:
Stand before a mirror, imperfections on full display. Deliver your comedy routine to yourself. Laugh, smile, and appreciate the distinctive quirks that make you authentically you. This is your personal comedy show, and you are the headlining act.

4. Share the Laughter:
If you're feeling adventurous, share your comedy routine with a friend or family member. Laughter is infectious, and embracing imperfections becomes even more empowering when shared. Remember, you're not alone in this comedy club of life.

Embracing imperfections isn't solely about finding humour in life's chaos; it's about unlocking the potency of authentic living. When you release the grip on perfection, you make room for genuine connections, self-love, and a plethora of laughter.

Consider imperfections as the seasoning in the recipe of your life —too much perfection, and things quickly become bland. So, spice it up, my fatigued friends! Embrace the quirks, the blunders, and the glorious mess that uniquely defines you.

Now, let's delve into vulnerability. It's akin to the secret sauce of authentic living. When you embrace imperfections, you're essentially saying, "Here I am, world, flaws and all." It's a vulnerable act, and vulnerability is where the true magic unfolds.

I once perceived vulnerability as a weakness, a susceptibility to judgment and criticism. However, vulnerability is your superpower. It's the key to authentic connections, profound relationships, and a life that resonates with your true self.

- The Vulnerability Journal -

Let's engage in a vulnerability exercise to tap into this superpower:
1. The Vulnerability Reflection:

Reflect on a moment in your life when you felt genuinely vulnerable. It could be a personal challenge, a difficult conversation, or a moment of self-doubt. Document the details— the emotions, the circumstances, and how it influenced you.

2. The Growth Spotlight:
Shift the focus from vulnerability as a weakness to vulnerability as a catalyst for growth. In your journal, explore how that vulnerable moment contributed to your personal development. Did it lead to self-discovery, resilience, or a shift in perspective?

3. The Vulnerability Affirmation:
Craft a vulnerability affirmation for yourself. It could be something like, "I embrace vulnerability as my superpower, opening doors to authentic connections and personal growth." Repeat this affirmation daily, reinforcing the strength that vulnerability brings into your life.

4. Share Your Story (Optional):
If you feel inclined, share your vulnerability reflection and affirmation with someone you trust. Whether it's a friend, family member, or a supportive online community, sharing your story can inspire others to embrace their vulnerabilities too.

Journal Prompts:

As you conclude this chapter, here are additional journal prompts to further explore the realms of your unfiltered authenticity:

1. What are three imperfections or quirks about myself that I can celebrate rather than criticise? How can embracing these imperfections contribute to a more authentic and joyful life?

2. Reflect on a time when you perceived vulnerability as a weakness. How did it shape your understanding of authenticity, and how can you redefine vulnerability as a strength in your life?

3. Consider a person you admire for their authenticity. What specific qualities or actions make them authentic, and how can you incorporate those elements into your own life?

Remember, imperfections are the strokes that paint the masterpiece of your story. They contribute to the uniqueness of your journey. So, let the quirks shine, laugh in the face of perfection, and pirouette through life with the liberating rhythm of your authentic self.

Letting Go of the Comparison Game: Celebrating Your Unique Journey

You know the drill – the endless scroll through social media, where everyone seems to have it all together while you're over here wondering if wearing two different socks counts as a fashion statement.

Let me tell you something: it's time to drop the comparison game. Seriously, just let it go like you're releasing a helium balloon into the wild. In this chapter, we're going to unravel the myth of perfection and embrace the glorious messiness of our unique journeys.

We live in a world of filters, curated feeds, and highlight reels that make everyone's life look like a never-ending vacation. Here's the truth bomb – it's all smoke and mirrors. Nobody has it together 24/7. I once tried to make avocado toast look as photogenic as those Instagram influencers – it ended up looking like a mushy green blob.

So, the first practical exercise is to conduct a social media detox. Unfollow those accounts that make you feel less-than. Create a space that uplifts you instead of triggering FOMO. Remember, comparison is the thief of joy, and we're in the business of joy restoration.

Life is messy. It's like trying to fold a fitted sheet – impossible. But here's the kicker – the beauty lies in the chaos. Let's embrace the comedy of errors that is our existence. I once accidentally wore my shirt inside out to a job interview. Did I get the job?

Surprisingly, yes. Life is unpredictable, and we need to learn to roll with the punches.

For our next exercise, I want you to think of a moment in your life when things went hilariously wrong. Did you spill coffee on your boss during a Zoom meeting? Share it! Write it down and revel in the absurdity of life. Laughter is a potent medicine, my friends.

Comparison not only happens online but also in the confines of our own minds. We constantly measure our success against others, forgetting that each journey is unique. It's like comparing apples to bowling balls – they're entirely different things. So, let's declutter that mental space.

Grab a pen and paper – we're going old school. List three accomplishments or moments you're proud of, no matter how small. Did you finally conquer the art of folding that fitted sheet? Celebrate it! Recognising your achievements, big or small, is crucial to breaking free from the comparison trap.

Now, let's talk about the acceptance anthem. **Repeat after me: "I am enough."** Say it loud and proud. In a world that constantly tells us we need to do more, be more, achieve more – it's time to acknowledge that we are inherently worthy just as we are. You don't need to keep up with the Joneses; you are the Joneses.

For our final exercise, write down three things that make you uniquely you. It could be your quirky sense of humour, your love for cheesy '80s movies, or your talent for doing the moonwalk in socks. Embrace your individuality and let go of the need to fit into someone else's mold.

- The Comparison Detox -

1. Social Media Cleanse:
Take a break from social media for a day. Instead of scrolling through highlight reels, spend that time doing something you genuinely enjoy – even if it's just staring at a wall. Trust me, it's more fulfilling.

2. Reality Check:
Make a list of the less-than-glamorous moments in your day. Forget where you parked your car? Perfect. Embrace the imperfections – they make life interesting.

3. Superhero Unplugged:
Identify your "superhero syndrome" moments. When do you feel the pressure to be superhuman? Jot them down and give yourself permission to let go of those unrealistic expectations.

Journal Prompts:

1. Reflect on a moment when social media made you feel inadequate. What steps can you take to create a more positive online space for yourself?

2. Share a funny story from your life where things didn't go as planned. How can you find humour in life's imperfections moving forward?

3. List three accomplishments, big or small, that you're proud of. How can you celebrate these achievements more often?

4. Repeat the acceptance anthem: "I am enough." How does this mantra make you feel, and how can you incorporate it into your daily life?

5. Write down three things that make you uniquely you. How can you embrace and celebrate these qualities without comparing yourself to others?

Remember, my tired but resilient friends, life is not a competition. It's a wild, messy, and beautiful journey uniquely yours. Let's revel in our imperfections, celebrate our victories, and continue embracing the power of acceptance.

Acceptance Amidst Chaos: Finding Calm in the Storm

Get ready because this chapter is your passport to inner calm amid life's uproar – and let me assure you, my life is a carnival of unexpected twists.

Picture this: I'm on a mission to conquer a mountain of paperwork, juggling phone calls, only to realise I forgot to pick up a crucial document for a meeting. Chaos ensues. I call this the

"Paperwork-Call-Meeting Tango" – a dance I never signed up for, yet it seems to be a recurring theme.

Life is an unpredictable adventure, and the sooner we embrace it, the smoother the ride. Trying to control every element is like trying to catch fireflies in a jar – delightful, but the notion of total capture is whimsical.

Acceptance isn't about surrender; it's recognising that life is a mosaic of unplanned events, occasionally wafting the aroma of a culinary experiment gone awry. It's about discovering serenity within the tempest, even when that whirlwind involves misplaced keys and surprise visits from your quirky neighbour while you're in your weekend PJs.

Now, let's dive into some hands-on exercises to nurture acceptance amidst life's vibrant tapestry:

- The Chaos Checklist -

1. Mindful Multitasking:
Choose one chaotic moment in your day, like cooking dinner while on a work call. Instead of stressing, immerse yourself fully in each task. Notice the sizzle of the pan, pay attention to the conversation. Embrace the chaos by being present in the moment.

2. Laugh Breaks:
Schedule "laugh breaks" throughout your day. Watch a funny video, listen to a comedy podcast, or recall a hilarious memory. Laughter is the ultimate acceptance tool – it turns chaos into comedy.

3. Breathe Through It:

When chaos strikes, pause for a moment. Take three deep breaths. Inhale the acceptance, exhale the stress. It's like a mini-vacation for your mind.

Life's narrative isn't a meticulously crafted masterpiece; think of it more as an uproarious comedy sketch with surprising twists. The quicker we welcome those quirks, the faster we can revel in the hilarity.

Ever noticed the infectious nature of laughter? It's like the joyful version of the flu. Unearthing humour in the midst of disorder isn't merely a skill; it's a survival strategy. My life mirrors a comedy series, and I've mastered the art of harmonising with the imaginary laughter track.

Once, I accidentally turned my orange juice into a laptop accessory right before a virtual meeting. Rather than succumbing to panic, I embraced the pandemonium. With a goofy expression, I proudly showcased my orange juice-stained keyboard like a contemporary art masterpiece.

- *Comedy Journal* -

1. Document the Chaos:

Keep a journal of chaotic moments throughout your week. Include everything from misplaced keys to accidentally wearing mismatched socks. The more ridiculous, the better.

2. Find the Funny:
For each chaotic entry, find something humorous about the situation. How can you turn these moments into comedic anecdotes? Remember, life is a comedy – you might as well enjoy the punchlines.

3. Share the Laughter:
Share your favourite chaotic moments with a friend or family member. Laughter loves company, and sharing these stories can turn chaos into a bonding experience.

Acceptance is not about waving a white flag; it's about surrendering to the beautiful mess that is life. Embracing chaos doesn't mean chaos wins – it means you're choosing peace over perfection.

- The Surrender Session -

1. Identify Control Triggers:
What situations trigger your need for control? Is it a messy house, unexpected interruptions, or last-minute changes to plans? Identify these triggers.

2. Surrender Ritual:
Create a ritual when faced with a control trigger. It could be a simple mantra, a deep breath, or even a symbolic gesture like opening your hands as a sign of letting go. Practice surrendering to the chaos in these moments.

3. Celebrate the Chaos:
Instead of resisting chaos, celebrate it. Throw a "Chaos Celebration" where you intentionally let go of control and embrace the unpredictability of life.

Journal Prompts:

1. How does your perception of chaos impact your stress levels?

2. What humorous aspect can you find in a recent chaotic situation?

3. In what areas of your life can you practice surrendering to the chaos and embracing imperfection?

Acceptance isn't about taming the chaos; it's about learning to dance in the rain of unpredictability. So, let's put on our acceptance tap shoes and gracefully navigate the storm, one chaotically perfect step at a time.

Unmasking Vulnerability: The Strength in Being Real

Hey fabulous acceptance aficionados! Grab your emotional snorkel because we're about to swim through the sea of feelings, and trust me, it's a wacky, unpredictable tide.

Vulnerability. It's like that weird cousin you avoid at family gatherings. We've all been there, thinking vulnerability is a sign of weakness. But, my friends, it's time to flip the script. Vulnerability isn't weakness; it's your superpower, your secret weapon against the dragons of self-doubt.

For the longest time, I thought vulnerability was like opening the floodgates to a sea of judgment. I mean, who wants to expose their soft underbelly to the world? But here's the kicker – vulnerability isn't about showcasing weaknesses; it's about showcasing authenticity.

If life were a comedy special, vulnerability would be the punchline that catches you off guard. I used to think vulnerability meant sharing your deepest, darkest secrets with the world, like a confessional booth on steroids. But vulnerability is more like sharing your awkward first date stories – a mix of cringe and charm.

Imagine this: I'm at a social gathering, attempting to be effortlessly cool, and I spill salsa all over myself. Instead of pretending it didn't happen, I embraced the tomato-stained disaster and made a joke about my new avant-garde salsa art.

Vulnerability turned a potential embarrassment into a hilarious moment that broke the ice.

- *The Vulnerability Victory List* -

1. Awkward Achievements:
Make a list of your awkward, embarrassing, or "I-can't-believe-that-just-happened" moments. It's time to celebrate the charm in your quirks.

2. Share the Silliness:
Pick one awkward achievement from your list and share it with a friend. Revel in the humour, and watch how vulnerability turns a mishap into a shared laugh.

3. Vulnerability Victory:
The next time you find yourself in an awkward situation, own it. Make a joke, laugh it off, and watch how vulnerability transforms the experience.

Life isn't a photoshopped Instagram feed; it's a raw, unfiltered documentary. We spend so much time curating the perfect image, fearing that our true selves aren't Instagram-worthy. But here's the truth – imperfections are the brushstrokes that make the masterpiece of your life.

Think about your favourite comedians. What makes them hilarious? It's not their flawless delivery; it's their ability to be real, to expose their vulnerabilities and turn them into relatable, gut-busting moments.

In my own life, I used to feel the need to present the polished version of Emily to the world – the one who had it all together, who never faced doubts or insecurities. But, oh boy, was that exhausting. It's like trying to carry a backpack full of rocks while wearing stilettos. Eventually, I embraced the power of realness. I let go of the need to be perfect and found strength in my authenticity.

- *The Realness Ritual* -

1. Authenticity Inventory:
Reflect on the parts of yourself you tend to hide or downplay. It could be your quirks, fears, or insecurities. Make a list and acknowledge them without judgment.

2. Authenticity Unleashed:
Choose one aspect from your authenticity inventory and let it shine. Share it with someone close to you, be it a friend or a family member. Witness how vulnerability transforms into a bridge connecting you on a deeper level.

3. Real Talk Challenge:
The next time you're in a conversation, resist the urge to present the polished version of yourself. Share a genuine thought, a true feeling, or a personal experience. Notice how being real creates a more authentic connection.

If life is a comedy, self-compassion is the punchline that turns self-criticism into a stand-up routine. We've all been there – the inner critic that's harsher than a food critic on a bad day. But, my friend, it's time to give yourself a standing ovation instead of an endless critique.

In the world of comedy, self-deprecating humour can be gold. It's like making fun of your own cooking skills – endearing and relatable. Similarly, self-compassion is the ability to laugh at your own quirks, mistakes, and imperfections without the harsh judgment.

- The Self-Compassion Comedy Club -

1. Critique to Comedy:
Identify one self-critique that's been playing on repeat in your mind. Now, turn it into a self-deprecating joke. It's time to lighten the mental load.

2. Laughter Meditation:
Spend five minutes a day reflecting on your day's challenges with a touch of humour. Imagine you're narrating the events in a comedy routine. Notice how laughter transforms your perspective.

3. Compassion Counter:
Create a tally system. Every time you catch yourself being self-critical, replace it with a self-compassionate thought or action. Let the laughter of self-kindness drown out the harsh critiques.

Journal Prompts:

1. How has the fear of vulnerability affected your interactions and relationships?

2. What are some aspects of yourself that you tend to hide or downplay? How can you embrace and celebrate these elements?

3. Describe a situation where you turned vulnerability into a moment of connection or laughter. What did you learn from that experience?

Remember, vulnerability is not the absence of strength; it's the revelation of it. So, let's unmask our vulnerabilities, embrace imperfections, and turn self-compassion into a hilarious routine. Your authenticity is your superpower, and the world deserves a front-row seat to the comedy that is uniquely you.

Navigating Life's Uncertainties: Embracing the Beauty of the Unknown

Buckle up because this chapter is all about manoeuvring through the maze of uncertainties – and trust me, life's uncertainties are like a game of Twister, only with more plot twists.

Life is like walking a tightrope blindfolded – exhilarating, terrifying, and occasionally resulting in a face-plant. The unknowns are like surprise guests at a party you didn't know you were hosting. For the longest time, I treated uncertainty like a pop quiz I didn't study for – panic mode activated.

But here's the twist – uncertainty isn't the enemy; it's the avant-garde artist of life's canvas. It's the unexpected plot twist that keeps the story interesting, like a movie that doesn't follow the predictable rom-com formula. Uncertainty is the wild card that adds depth to the storyline of your life.

Raise your hand if you've ever fallen into the trap of certainty addiction. You know, that insatiable desire to have a foolproof plan for every aspect of your life. Guilty as charged! I used to think having a step-by-step plan was the key to a stress-free existence. Life had other plans, and they were often more hilarious than my meticulously crafted ones.

Certainty addiction is like trying to control a wild pack of squirrels – entertaining to watch, but utterly futile. Life doesn't come with a GPS, and that's the beauty of it. It's a choose-your-own-adventure novel, and the uncertainty is what makes each page turn exciting.

- The Certainty Detox -

1. Plan B Bonanza:
Identify a recent situation where your original plan went out the window. Now, jot down three unexpected positive outcomes that arose from the uncertainty. It's time to celebrate the unplanned victories.

2. Spontaneity Sprint:
Designate a day where you throw caution to the wind and embrace the unknown. Let go of your need for plans and allow spontaneity to be your guide. It could be a random adventure, trying a new cuisine, or even taking a different route to work.

3. Gratitude for the Unscripted:
Each evening, reflect on one thing that unfolded unexpectedly during your day. Find gratitude in the beauty of the unscripted moments, recognising that sometimes the best scenes are the unplanned ones.

Acceptance isn't just about embracing the known; it's about cozying up to the mystery of the unknown. It's like being on a blind date with life – you have no idea what's coming, but you're open to the possibility that it might be surprisingly delightful.

I used to fear the unknown like it was a haunted house, anticipating monsters behind every uncertainty. But, lo and behold, life's uncertainties turned out to be more like mischievous sprites than terrifying creatures. Embracing the mystery doesn't mean having all the answers; it means finding joy in the journey of discovery.

Trying to control the uncontrollable is like herding cats – an amusing but futile endeavour. I once attempted to plan every detail of a family vacation, from the itinerary to bathroom breaks. Guess what happened? The universe unleashed its comedic genius, throwing unexpected detours and hilarious misadventures my way. Lesson learned: life is the ultimate improv show, and trying to control it is like shared laughter. You'll be amazed at how humour transforms uncertainties into memorable anecdotes.

Acceptance isn't a passive surrender to the unknown; it's an active embrace of life's unpredictable dance. It's like stepping onto the dance floor without knowing the next move, but trusting that every step, whether smooth or stumbled, adds to the rhythm of your unique journey.

I used to dread uncertainty, treating it like an unwanted guest overstaying its welcome. But the more I tried to kick it out, the more it lingered. It wasn't until I invited uncertainty to sit at the table, offering it a cup of tea, that I realised it wasn't the enemy; it was a quirky companion adding flavour to the journey.

Life's uncertainties are like dance partners; they might step on your toes, but they also lead you to unexpected choreography. Acceptance is a dynamic dance where you learn to sway with the rhythm of the unknown.

- The Dance of Acceptance -

1. Dance Floor Visualisation:
Close your eyes and imagine yourself on a dance floor. Picture uncertainties as dance partners. Allow yourself to move with the flow, embracing the twists and turns.

2. The Acceptance Waltz:
Choose one area of uncertainty in your life. Instead of resisting or fearing it, waltz with it. See how your perspective changes when you allow acceptance to guide your steps.

3. Rhythm Reflection:
After an uncertain situation, reflect on the rhythm of your response. Did you resist, or did you allow acceptance to lead the dance? Notice how embracing the unknown can shift your emotional dance moves.

Journal Prompts:

1. How has the fear of uncertainties impacted your decision-making and overall well-being?

2. Think of a past situation where uncertainty turned out to be a positive force. How did your perspective change once the outcome unfolded?

3. Describe a recent moment when you resisted uncertainty. How might the situation have unfolded differently if you had embraced the unknown with acceptance?

Remember, life's uncertainties are the spice in the grand recipe of your existence. By embracing the beauty of the unknown, you're not just dancing through uncertainties; you're choreographing a unique and vibrant life story. So, lace up those metaphorical dance shoes, twirl with the uncertainties, and let acceptance lead you in the rhythm of the unpredictable. After all, the beauty of the unknown is often where life's most enchanting melodies play.

The Art of Forgiveness: Freeing Yourself from Resentment

Hey there, tired souls! Emily here, ready to dive into a topic that might seem a bit counterintuitive when you're already feeling worn out – forgiveness. Yeah, I know, who has the energy for that, right? But bear with me; this is where the magic happens.

Now, before you roll your eyes and think, "Oh great, another self-help guru telling me to forgive and forget," let me assure you – I get it. Forgiveness isn't about letting others off the hook for their actions; it's about releasing the grip resentment has on your precious energy. It's like decluttering your mental space but instead of old sweaters, you're tossing out grudges.

Let's be real – holding onto resentment is like drinking poison and expecting the other person to die. I used to be the queen of holding grudges. Someone would cut in line at the grocery store, and I'd be plotting their downfall for days. But guess what? All that seething rage did nothing but drain my already limited energy reserves.

So, I decided to approach forgiveness with the same sassiness I bring to a stand-up comedy routine. Picture this: me, a spotlight, and a mic, dropping punchlines about letting go of grudges. Trust me, laughter is the best medicine, especially when it comes to dealing with the ridiculousness of holding onto resentment.

- The Forgiveness Fiesta -

1. Write a Resentment Roast:
Take a piece of paper and jot down all the things that tick you off. Be as detailed and dramatic as you want. Then, read it aloud like you're performing a comedy special – the angrier, the better. Bonus points for funny voices!

2. Flip the Script:
Now, turn the script. Imagine the person who irks you has a quirky backstory or a ridiculous reason for their actions. It's like creating a character in a sitcom. Remember, you're the scriptwriter, and you get to decide how the story unfolds.

3. Laughter Meditation:
Find a quiet spot, close your eyes, and visualise yourself laughing at the absurdity of holding onto grudges. Picture it like a sitcom audience laughing track. Let the laughter wash away the

resentment. Because, let's face it, life is too short for unnecessary drama.

Forgiveness isn't only about others; it's also about cutting yourself some slack. If you're anything like me, you've got a laundry list of self-criticisms, a mental highlight reel of every mistake you've ever made. Well, it's time to hit the stop button on that endless loop.

- Mirror Pep Talk -

1. Stand in Front of the Mirror:
Look yourself in the eye. Yes, I know, it feels weird, but we're doing this.

2. Compliment Yourself:
Start with something simple. Maybe it's the way you always make the perfect cup of coffee or the fact that you remembered to feed your plants. Celebrate the small victories.

3. Forgive Your Imperfections:
Speak aloud about a mistake or flaw you've been beating yourself up over. Acknowledge it, then forgive yourself. Remember, you're a work in progress, not a finished masterpiece.

Journal Prompts:

1. What grudges or resentments am I holding onto that are draining my energy?

2. How can I incorporate humour into my forgiveness practice to make it more enjoyable?

3. What's one thing I can forgive myself for today?

4. In what ways can I infuse more laughter into my life to combat resentment?

Forgiveness isn't a sign of weakness; it's a demonstration of strength. So, let go of that resentment baggage, reclaim your energy, and get ready to live a life filled with more laughter and less drama.

Mindful Living: Finding Serenity in the Present Moment

I bring you a topic that's all about slowing down and savouring life like it's a decadent piece of chocolate cake – mindful living. Now, I know what you're thinking: "Mindful? In this chaotic circus called life?" Trust me, I get it. Please be patient with me; this isn't about joining a monastery or meditating on a mountain. We're talking about injecting a dose of Zen into our everyday craziness.

Let me paint you a picture. I used to be the queen of multitasking – answering emails while cooking, planning my week during a Netflix binge, and attempting to meditate with one eye open. It wasn't working. My life felt like a symphony of honking horns, and I was the conductor desperately trying to maintain some semblance of order.

Enter mindful living, the superhero cape we all need to navigate this chaotic city of life. It's not about shutting off your thoughts or pretending you're on a deserted island. No, it's about embracing the present moment – honking horns and all – with a dash of humour and a sprinkle of acceptance.

- The Multitasking Mania Mixer -

1. Choose a Mundane Task:
Pick something you do on autopilot, like washing dishes, folding laundry, or commuting (safely, of course). This isn't the time to attempt mind-bending tasks. We're starting small.

2. Engage Your Senses:
Instead of zoning out or daydreaming, tune into your senses. Feel the water temperature on your hands, notice the texture of the fabric, or appreciate the rhythm of your footsteps.

3. Inject Humour:
Turn it into a comedy routine. Imagine you're a stand-up comic doing a set about the absurdity of folding fitted sheets or the deep philosophical thoughts your toaster might be having.

Mindful living isn't about escaping the chaos; it's about dancing in the rain of life's craziness. I've learned that the more I resist the chaos, the more chaotic it gets. It's like trying to catch a handful of water – the tighter you grip, the more slips through your fingers.

- *Chaos Acceptance Dance Party* -

1. Crank Up the Tunes:
Pick a lively song that gets your feet tapping. Imagine your chaos as dance partners. They might have clumsy moves, but hey, they're part of the dance of life.

2. Dance with Abandon:
Move your body like no one's watching. As you dance, visualise embracing the chaos around you – the missed deadlines, the spilled coffee, the unpredictable twists and turns.

3. Laugh It Out:
If you step on your cat's tail or knock over a plant, laugh it off. Life's a dance, not a perfectly choreographed routine. Embrace the messiness, and let the laughter be your rhythm.

One area where mindfulness can revolutionise your life is in the world of snacking. I used to inhale my snacks like they were about to disappear. Then, I realised there's a whole universe of flavour waiting to be savoured.

- Snack Savasana -

1. Choose a Snack:
Pick something you enjoy – it could be a piece of chocolate, a handful of almonds, or even a juicy apple.

2. Set the Scene:
Find a quiet spot. Turn off distractions. This is your snack sanctuary.

3. Engage Your Senses:
Before taking a bite, notice the colour, texture, and aroma. Take a moment to appreciate the masterpiece in your hands.

4. Bite Mindfully:
Take a small bite and savour the flavours. Close your eyes if it helps you focus. Let the taste linger before taking another bite.

5. Reflect with a Smile:
How often do we rush through snacks without truly enjoying them? Take a moment to reflect on the experience. Who knew mindful snacking could be this satisfying?

Journal Prompts:

1. What aspects of my daily life do I find challenging to be present for?

2. How can I inject humour into the chaos of my everyday routine?

3. What are three small, mundane tasks I can turn into opportunities for mindful living this week?

4. In what ways can I embrace the chaos and dance with it instead of resisting?

Remember, my lovely warriors of whimsy, mindful living is your ticket to finding serenity in the present moment. So, slow down, laugh a little, and savour the deliciousness of life, one mindful moment at a time.

Letting Go of Control: Surrendering to Life's Flow

Embarking on the labyrinthine journey of embracing acceptance is akin to skill fully juggling not just flaming torches but an entire arsenal of dynamic elements. Allow me to recount my personal saga as the erstwhile captain of the control-freak ship, steering it with unwavering determination straight into the tumultuous storm of stress. The echoes of that turbulent voyage serve as a testament to the misconceptions surrounding control and the transformative power of acceptance. Today, we embark on a profound exploration, unraveling the layers of this intricate journey, as we cultivate an intimate relationship with chaos and gracefully submit to the capricious choreography that is life.

Imagine this: a version of myself meticulously regulating every conceivable aspect of existence, from the seemingly mundane act of folding towels with precision to crafting a detailed itinerary that left no room for spontaneity. In the throes of this misguided pursuit, I erroneously believed that control was synonymous with power. I clung to the illusion that the tighter I held on, the more assertive my command over life's unfolding narrative would be. Little did I realise the fallacy in this belief.

Life, I discovered, is an elaborate improvisational show, devoid of a preordained script and absent of any rehearsals. It is an unscripted spectacle, a grand stage upon which the unforeseen takes centre stage. In my quest for control, I had failed to grasp the fundamental truth that the essence of life lies in its inherent unpredictability.

The metaphorical torches I attempted to juggle were not just fiery symbols of challenges, but dynamic representations of the myriad elements that constitute our existence — relationships, career aspirations, personal goals, and the ever-elusive concept of time. Acceptance, it turns out, is not a defeat; rather, it is a courageous acknowledgment that the grand tapestry of life is woven with threads of uncertainty and spontaneity.

As we delve deeper into this profound exploration, we unravel the transformative potential inherent in accepting the unpredictable dance of life. It involves releasing the tight grip on the illusion of control and opening ourselves to the beauty of the unknown. This acceptance is not a passive resignation but an active participation in the unfolding drama, embracing the twists and turns with a newfound sense of freedom.

In conclusion, the journey of letting go and accepting life's flow is not just about relinquishing control but understanding that true power lies in our ability to navigate the unpredictable currents with resilience and grace. It is an ongoing process of self-discovery, a journey that invites us to release the reins and allow the symphony of life to serenade us with its unrestrained melody.

- *Control Freak Comedy Roast* -

1. Write a Control Manifesto:
Grab a piece of paper and list all the things you try to control in your life. Be brutally honest – even if it includes attempting to control the weather (we've all been there).

2. Turn It into a Stand-Up Routine:
Take your manifesto and turn it into a comedy routine. Imagine you're performing at a comedy club, poking fun at the absurdity of trying to control everything. Laughter is your superpower here.

3. Share the Laughter:
If you feel comfortable, share your routine with a friend or family member. Sometimes, laughter shared is a step towards letting go.

So, how do we shift from control freak to life's improv troupe member? The key, my exhausted amigos, lies in acceptance. It's about acknowledging that life's script is more of a suggestion than a strict guideline.

- Surrender Cinema Night -

1. Choose a Movie:
Pick a film where the protagonist learns to let go or navigate unexpected twists with grace. Classic choices include "Eat Pray Love," "The Secret Life of Walter Mitty," or even "Frozen" – because, let's face it, Elsa totally nailed the whole letting go thing.

2. Watch with Intention:
As you watch, pay attention to how the characters handle moments of uncertainty. Observe their journey of surrendering to the flow of life.

3. Reflect and Relate:
After the movie, reflect on your own life. In what areas can you embrace a more flexible, go-with-the-flow attitude? Bonus points if you can find humour in the chaos.

Life is a wild river, and we're all navigating in makeshift rafts. Instead of desperately gripping the sides, what if we let the current guide us? Sounds terrifying, right? But trust me, it's where the magic happens.

- The Uncertainty River Cruise -

1. Draw Your Raft:
On a piece of paper, draw a little raft. Label it with areas of your life where you're holding onto control for dear life.

2. Colour Outside the Lines:
Literally! Use bright colours to doodle chaos around your raft. Embrace the messiness, because life's canvas is never a neat colouring book.

3. Cut the Anchor:
Identify one aspect you're ready to release control over. It could be as simple as letting someone else take charge of dinner plans or not meticulously planning every minute of your weekend.

Journal Prompts:

1. What areas of my life do I feel the need to control, and how does it impact my energy levels?

2. How can I infuse humour into moments of uncertainty to make them more manageable?

3. What is one small step I can take today to let go of control in a specific area of my life?

4. In what ways can surrendering to life's flow bring more joy and spontaneity into my daily routine?

Letting go of control doesn't mean giving up power; it's about gaining the freedom to enjoy the unpredictable journey of life. So, release those metaphorical reins, laugh in the face of chaos, and let life's improv show surprise and delight you.

Acceptance: The Unlikely Superpower

Welcome to the acceptance party – no, not the kind where we accept invitations, but the one where we accept the chaos that is life with open arms and a hint of sass. In this chapter, we're diving headfirst into the magical world of acceptance, the kind that turns exhaustion into energy and fatigue into fabulousness.

Let's kick things off with a reality check. Life is like a carnival game, and we're all just trying to navigate the chaos without dropping our cotton candy. Acceptance is your golden ticket to winning this game with style. It's not about throwing in the towel; it's about embracing the mess while looking fabulous doing it.

Now, you might be wondering, "Emily, how do I even begin to accept the madness that is my life?" Fear not, my weary friend, for I am here to spill the acceptance tea.

First things first – let's talk about self-talk. We all have that little voice in our heads that either cheers us on or drags us down like a wet blanket. Picture this: you're slogging through another hectic day, and that inner critic starts whispering sweet nothings like, "You're not doing enough," or "You should be Super(wo)man, not Super-tired person."

Well, it's time to kick that negative Nancy out of your mental space and welcome in the voice of reason – you! Practice the art of positive self-talk. When the inner critic starts its tirade, shut it down with statements like, **"I accept that today is a bit much, and that's okay,"** or **"I am doing my best, and that is more than enough."**

Shifting your mindset to acceptance is like switching from a black and white TV to Technicolor. Suddenly, the world seems brighter, and you start seeing opportunities instead of obstacles. It's not about pretending everything is sunshine and rainbows; it's about acknowledging the storms and dancing in the rain.

Another nifty trick in the acceptance toolkit is the **"I Am"** statements. These are like little affirmations that pack a punch. When you catch yourself spiralling into the abyss of self-doubt, repeat after me, **"I am tired, and that's okay,"** or **"I am not lazy; I am human, damn it!"** It's a simple yet powerful way to rewire your brain and embrace the reality of your feelings.

Now, let's talk about the grandmaster move of acceptance – letting go of the need for perfection. I know, I know, it's easier said than done. But trust me, perfection is an illusion, and it's time to shatter that glass slipper. Acceptance means understanding that it's okay to have a messy house, to miss a deadline, or to rock yesterday's socks because, well, laundry can wait.

Give yourself permission to be beautifully imperfect. Picture this as your official permission slip: **"I, [Your Name], hereby grant myself the right to be gloriously imperfect and accept that life is messy, and that's perfectly fine."** Go ahead, sign it – I'll wait.

Acceptance is not about resignation; it's about acknowledging the reality of your situation without letting it define you. It's like saying, **"Hey, life, you might throw curveballs, but I've got an acceptance bat, and I'm ready to hit them out of the park."** Who knew accepting reality could be so empowering?

Oh, and here's a secret – acceptance is contagious. Once you start embracing the chaos with open arms, you'll notice the people around you doing the same. It's like starting a revolution of fabulous fatigue fighters, and you, my friend, are the fearless leader.

In conclusion, acceptance is not a one-size-fits-all cape; it's a tailored suit that you wear with pride. So, my tired but fabulous comrades, let's raise a toast to acceptance, the unlikely superpower that transforms the ordinary into the extraordinary. Life might be a carnival, but with acceptance, you're not just a spectator – you're the star of the show. Own it, accept it, and watch as your vitality comes roaring back like a superhero on a caffeine high.

Because Even Tired Souls Deserve a Little Sunshine

Now, I know what you're thinking – "Emily, in the midst of my chaotic life, how on earth am I supposed to summon gratitude?" Well, grab your gratitude goggles because we're about to turn those weary eyes into windows of appreciation.

Let's talk about gratitude in its purest, unfiltered form – the art of saying "Thank You." It's not just about mouthing the words; it's about truly feeling the thankfulness deep within your soul. So, next time someone holds the door for you, or your friend sends you a hilarious meme, channel your inner Adele and say, "Thank you from the other side!" Bonus points if you throw in some jazz hands.

Let's get a little deeper. I call this exercise **"Gratitude Journaling for the Slightly Sassy Soul."** Get yourself a journal – the funkier, the better – and make it your gratitude sanctuary. Each day, jot down three things you're thankful for. It could be as simple as the barista getting your coffee order right or as profound as finally mastering the art of adulting (because let's be real, adulting is hard).

But here's the twist – add a dash of humour to your entries. Turn your gratitude journal into a stand-up routine. For example, "Today, I am grateful for my coffee, because without it, I'd be a grumpy unicorn. Cheers to you, magical bean juice!"

Next up, let's sprinkle some gratitude confetti on your relationships. Take a moment to appreciate the people in your life, even the ones who leave the toilet seat up or borrow your favourite sweater without asking (you know who you are). Write a little thank-you note – virtual or handwritten, your call – expressing your gratitude for their quirks and all. Trust me, it's like giving your relationships a warm, fuzzy sweater of appreciation.

Now, let's talk about the power of **"Gratitude Reminders."** Set up little cues throughout your day to prompt gratitude. It could be a reminder on your phone, a sticky note on your mirror, or even a quirky alarm sound that makes you smile. When that reminder pops up, take a minute to pause and reflect on something you're thankful for. It's like a mini-vacation for your soul, without the need for a suitcase.

Oh, and let's not forget the **"Gratitude Swap"** – an activity that turns your usual complaints into moments of thankfulness. The next time you catch yourself grumbling about traffic or the weather, flip the script. Instead, find something positive in the situation. Stuck in traffic? Well, it's the perfect time for a solo dance party in your car. Rainy day? Embrace it and channel your inner Gene Kelly – you're practically singing in the rain.

Now, here's a game-changer – the **"Gratitude Playlist."** Create a playlist of songs that make your heart do a happy dance. It could be anything from '90s pop hits to classical symphonies – whatever gets your toes tapping. Play it whenever you need a gratitude boost. Trust me, dancing like nobody's watching is an instant mood lifter.

Lastly, let's talk about the grand finale – **"Gratitude Meditation."** Find a quiet space, sit comfortably, and close your eyes. Take a few deep breaths, and with each exhale, release any tension. Now, visualise three things you're grateful for. Picture them in vivid detail, immerse yourself in the feelings they evoke, and let that warm, fuzzy gratitude envelop you like a cozy blanket.

Journal prompts:

1. Reflect on a recent challenging situation. How can you find a silver lining or something to be thankful for in that experience?

2. List three people in your life who have made a positive impact on you. Write a short thank-you note to each of them, expressing your gratitude.

3. Share a humorous entry from your gratitude journal. How did infusing humour into your gratitude practice affect your perspective?

4. Describe a "Gratitude Reminder" that resonates with you. How does incorporating these reminders into your day impact your overall mindset?

5. Choose a situation where you'd typically complain. How can you flip the script and find something to be thankful for in that scenario?

Remember, gratitude is like glitter – sprinkle it generously, and watch as your world transforms into a dazzling masterpiece. Stay fabulous, stay grateful, and let that tired soul of yours bask in the warmth of appreciation. You've got this!

Celebrating Small Wins: Acknowledging Your Progress

In the grand tapestry of conquering fatigue, there's a thread we often overlook – the small wins. Today, we're diving into the art of celebrating those victories, no matter how tiny they may seem. It's the secret sauce to reclaiming vitality.

Imagine running a marathon – a marathon of overcoming exhaustion, self-doubt, and societal pressures. It's a tough race, and sometimes, the finish line seems miles away. But here's the catch: every step you take, every hurdle you clear, deserves applause. Even the tiniest victories contribute to the grand symphony of reclaiming vitality.

- *Victory Vignettes* -

1. Create Your Win Scrapbook:
Grab a notebook or use a digital tool. Start documenting your small wins – finished a work task, resisted the urge to overcommit, or simply got out of bed when it felt impossible.

2. Illustrate with Emojis and Doodles:
Embrace your inner artist. Use emojis, doodles, or even stickers to illustrate your victories. Make it a visual feast that sparks joy.

3. Review and Revel:
Regularly flip through your scrapbook. Revel in the visual representation of your triumphs. It's a living testament to your resilience.

Now, let's talk about acceptance in the context of celebrating your wins. It's about acknowledging that progress, no matter how small, is still progress.

- Mini Victory Toast Ceremony -

1. Pick a Beverage:
It could be a cup of tea, a fizzy soda, or even a mocktail. Treat yourself – this is your victory elixir.

2. Designate a Celebration Spot:
Find a cozy corner or a spot with a view. This is your victory podium.

3. Toast to Your Triumphs:
Raise your beverage high and toast to your recent victories. Verbalise your acknowledgment of your progress – a mini ceremony just for you.

Gratitude is like the glitter that enhances the sparkle of your small wins. It adds an extra layer of joy and appreciation to your journey.

- Gratitude Journaling -

1. Daily Wins Journal:
Dedicate a section in your journal to jot down your daily wins. They could be as simple as having a moment of peace or finishing a chapter of a book.

2. Express Gratitude:
Alongside your wins, express gratitude for the circumstances or people that contributed to those victories. It could be as straightforward as thanking yourself for showing up.

3. Weekly Reflection:
At the end of the week, reflect on your gratitude entries. Notice how celebrating wins with gratitude transforms your perspective.

Life's journey is riddled with comedic moments, and your victories deserve a good laugh. Humour is the cherry on top of your celebratory sundae.

- Victory Comedy Night -

1. Compile a Funny Playlist:
Create a playlist of your favourite funny songs or stand-up routines. Laughter is the soundtrack to your victories.

2. Share Laughs with a Friend:
Call up a friend or family member. Share your small wins and enjoy a laughter-filled conversation. Laughter is contagious!

3. Joke About Your Milestones:
Create jokes or funny anecdotes about your recent victories. It could be as silly as, "I deserve a gold medal for adulting today."

Journal Prompts:

1. What small wins have I achieved recently that deserve acknowledgment?

2. How does celebrating small victories contribute to my overall sense of well-being?

3. In what ways can I infuse humour into my celebration of wins to make it more enjoyable?

4. What is one small goal I can set for myself, and how will I celebrate when I achieve it?

Celebrating small wins is not about the destination; it's about revealing in the journey. So, raise your imaginary or real glass to the victories, laugh in the face of challenges, and let the celebration of your triumphs be the melody that propels you forward.

Acceptance in Relationships: Nurturing Connection Through Understanding

Greetings, you magnificent architect of relationships! We embark on a profound exploration of the dance that is love and connection, equipped with the invaluable tool of acceptance. Brace yourself as we navigate the complex waters of relationships, where humour is our guiding star and acceptance serves as the unyielding anchor grounding us in the storm.

In the intricate tapestry of relationships, acceptance is not merely a passive acknowledgment of differences; it is an active and dynamic force that fosters understanding, cultivates resilience, and fortifies the very foundation of human connection.

Acceptance, in its essence, is the art of embracing the entirety of your partner – quirks, imperfections, idiosyncrasies, and all. It transcends the superficial layers of love, going beyond the initial euphoria of infatuation. It is a profound acknowledgment that your partner is a beautifully flawed human being, just like you, navigating the unpredictable journey of life.

At the heart of acceptance lies the willingness to let go of unrealistic expectations and to celebrate the uniqueness of your partner. It involves understanding that love is not a flawless fairy tale but a dynamic, evolving narrative filled with twists, turns, and occasional plot twists. Acceptance is the bridge that connects two individuals, allowing them to traverse the ups and downs of life hand in hand.

Picture acceptance as a multifaceted gem, with each facet representing a different aspect of its impact on relationships. One facet gleams with the power to defuse conflicts, turning potential battlegrounds into fertile grounds for understanding. Another facet reflects the resilience it instills, enabling relationships to weather the storms of life with grace and unity.

Moreover, acceptance is not a one-size-fits-all concept; it is a tailor-made garment that adjusts to the unique contours of each relationship. It involves actively listening to your partner's needs, concerns, and aspirations without judgment. It is a collaborative effort to create a safe haven where both individuals can express themselves authentically, free from the fear of rejection.

Now, let's delve into the practical exercises that can transform acceptance from a concept into a lived reality within the context of your relationship:

1. The Acceptance Cocktail:
Craft a mindset mixology by blending equal parts understanding, patience, and a splash of humour. When faced with a situation that tests your patience, take a metaphorical sip of your acceptance cocktail. Instead of reacting impulsively, respond with empathy and an open heart.

2. Expectation Limbo:
Visualise your expectations as limbo sticks – the lower, the better. Challenge yourself to lower the limbo stick when it comes to expectations of your partner. This exercise encourages you to approach your relationship with a more realistic and grounded perspective.

3. The Acceptance Diary:

Transform a notebook into your very own "Acceptance Diary." Chronicle moments where acceptance triumphed over frustration or misunderstanding. By documenting these instances, you create a tangible reminder of the progress made on your journey toward a more accepting relationship.

4. Love Language Decoder:

Become fluent in the language of your partner's heart. Identify their love language and make a conscious effort to communicate in a way that resonates with them. This exercise encourages a deeper understanding of each other's needs and strengthens the emotional connection.

5. The Apology Aikido:

Master the art of a sincere apology during conflicts. Instead of focusing on assigning blame, practice acknowledging the impact of your actions on your partner. Apologise not just for specific actions but also for the emotions those actions may have caused.

6. Humour Haven:

Create a shared space where humour is celebrated. Share funny anecdotes, memes, or jokes that lighten the mood. Laughter can be a powerful bonding agent, helping both partners navigate challenges with a lighter heart.

7. Conflict Acceptance:

View conflicts as opportunities for growth rather than threats to the relationship. Approach disagreements with a mindset of acceptance, understanding that differences are a natural part of any relationship. Seek compromise and common ground, fostering a sense of unity.

Journal prompts:

1. Reflect on a recent situation where acceptance played a crucial role in diffusing tension. How did embracing acceptance impact the outcome?

2. Share a humorous entry from your "Acceptance Diary." How has humour helped you navigate the quirks and idiosyncrasies of your partner?

3. Explore your partner's love language. How can you incorporate their love language into your daily interactions to deepen connection and understanding?

4. Describe a situation where you successfully executed "The Apology Aikido." How did a sincere apology contribute to resolving the conflict?

5. Reflect on the role of humour in your relationship. Share a memorable moment where laughter turned a challenging situation into a bonding experience.

In the grand tapestry of relationships, acceptance is the golden thread that weaves moments of joy, challenges, and growth into a resilient and beautiful connection. It is an ongoing journey, a commitment to understanding, and a celebration of the unique dance that is love. So, embrace the chaos, find humour in the journey, and let acceptance be the guiding force in your labyrinth of love. You're not just a relationship navigator; you're the captain of a ship destined for extraordinary adventures. Set sail with acceptance as your compass, and let the winds of love carry you to new horizons.

Breaking Free from Expectations: Rediscovering Joy on Your Terms

We're about to tackle the expectation monster that's been lurking in the shadows of your life, ready to pounce and sabotage your joy. We're not just facing it; we're wrestling it to the ground with a mix of humour, sass, and, of course, a generous dose of acceptance. So, buckle up, because we're on a journey to rediscover joy on your own terms.

Let's start with a hard truth – expectations are like those clingy exes who just won't leave you alone. They follow you around, whispering sweet nothings in your ear, and then, BAM! Reality check hits, and you're left wondering why you let them crash your party.

Here's the thing: expectations often come from external sources – society, family, that nosy neighbour who thinks they know everything about your life. It's time to grab those expectations by the horns and show them who's boss. It's you, with your newfound acceptance superpowers.

1. The Expectation Cleanse:
Imagine expectations as unwanted houseguests. Take a moment to identify the expectations lingering in your mental living room. Are they yours, or did someone else sneak them in? Write them down, crumple that list, and ceremoniously throw it in the metaphorical trash.

2. The Joyful Rebellion:
Picture yourself as the rebellious hero in your favourite action movie. Your mission? Break free from the chains of expectations. Identify one societal or familial expectation that's been holding you hostage, and devise a plan to rebel against it. It could be as simple as refusing to apologise for being authentically you. Channel your inner maverick and let the rebellion begin!

3. Expectation Vs. Reality Board:
Create a visual representation of your expectations versus reality. Draw a line down the middle of a piece of paper. On one side, list your expectations, and on the other, jot down the reality. Embrace the differences, and let this exercise be a reminder that reality is where the magic happens.

4. The "No" Challenge:
Practice saying "no" without guilt. Start small – maybe it's declining that extra project at work or turning down an invitation that you're not excited about. As you flex your "no" muscle, notice the liberating feeling that comes with putting your own well-being first.

5. Joyful Journaling:
Begin a joy journal where you document moments of pure happiness on your terms. It could be as simple as enjoying a cup of coffee in solitude or belting out your favourite song in the car. This journal is your personal joy manifesto, a testament to the joy you create outside the realm of expectations.

6. The Unfiltered Bucket List:
Create a bucket list, but here's the twist – make it entirely about what brings you joy, not what society tells you should be on it. Maybe it's learning to juggle, starting a quirky hobby, or traveling

to a place that's off the beaten path. Let this list be a celebration of your unique desires.

7. Unplugged Acceptance:
Designate a day to unplug from social media and external influences. During this day, focus on activities that genuinely bring you joy without the pressure of comparison or societal expectations. It's like a mini-vacation for your soul.

Breaking free from expectations is not a one-time event; it's a rebellious journey. Let me share a little secret – joy often hides in the unexpected, the uncharted territories where expectations fear to tread. When you accept that joy can be found in the unconventional, the ordinary becomes extraordinary.

Journal prompts:

1. Reflection on Expectations: List three expectations that have been weighing on your mind. How have these expectations influenced your choices and actions? Reflect on the origins of these expectations.

2. Joyful Rebellion: Share your experience with the "Joyful Rebellion" exercise. How did breaking free from an expectation make you feel? What actions can you take to continue rebelling against limiting expectations?

3. Expectation Vs. Reality Reflection: Examine your Expectation Vs. Reality Board. Were there any surprises or insights? How can you navigate the gaps between expectations and reality with acceptance and humour?

4. The "No" Challenge: Describe a situation where you practiced saying "no" without guilt. How did it impact your well-being? Reflect on any shifts in your mindset or sense of empowerment.

5. Joyful Journaling: Share a joyful moment you documented in your Joy Journal. How did this moment deviate from societal expectations? How can you incorporate more of these moments into your daily life?

6. Unfiltered Bucket List: List three items from your Unfiltered Bucket List. What makes these activities uniquely joyful for you? How can you prioritise incorporating them into your life?

7. Unplugged Acceptance: Reflect on your experience during the day of unplugging. How did disconnecting from external influences impact your sense of joy and acceptance? What activities brought you genuine happiness?

Remember, rediscovering joy on your terms is a rebellious act of self-love. Embrace the unexpected, relish in the unconventional, and let acceptance be the guiding light on your joyous journey. You're not just breaking free from expectations; you're rewriting the script of your own happiness. So, gear up for the adventure, laugh in the face of expectations, and let the joy rebellion begin!

Releasing Regret: Embracing the Lessons of the Past

Now, we're delving into the murky waters of regret. Yes, those pesky little ghosts of our past decisions that love to haunt our minds like an overly attached ex. But fear not, because we're not just going to face them; we're going to give them a makeover, turn them into life coaches, and, most importantly, show them the door with a sprinkle of humour and a hefty dose of acceptance.

Regret – it's like that unwanted souvenir you got from a questionable vacation. You didn't ask for it, and it certainly doesn't spark joy. But regret can be a wise teacher, not just a constant reminder of what could've been. So, grab your imaginary regret repellant and join me on this journey of releasing regret and embracing the lessons of the past.

1. The Regret Revue:
Imagine your regrets as characters in a theatrical production. Give each regret a role, a backstory, and maybe even a quirky costume. By turning your regrets into a comedy show, you're taking away their power to drag you down. Bonus points if you can throw in a musical number.

2. Acceptance Time Capsule:
Find a small box or container and dub it your "Acceptance Time Capsule." Write down a few regrets on separate pieces of paper, acknowledging the lessons they taught you. Fold them up, put them in the capsule, and bury it in a metaphorical backyard. This exercise symbolises your acceptance of the past and your commitment to moving forward.

3. The Regret Interview:

Picture yourself as a talk show host, and your regrets are the celebrity guests. Conduct a regret interview, asking each regret what it has taught you. It's like turning your regrets into wisdom-dropping guests on your very own show. Cue the imaginary applause!

4. Letter to Your Past Self:

Grab a pen and write a letter to your past self, specifically addressing a regret or two. Offer words of comfort, understanding, and a gentle reminder that mistakes are the stepping stones to growth. This exercise allows you to bridge the gap between your past and present with compassion.

5. Regretful Art Therapy:

Express your regrets through art. Whether it's painting, drawing, or sculpting with Play-Doh, let your creativity flow. Transform the negative energy of regret into a tangible piece of art that represents acceptance and growth.

6. The "Should've, Could've, Would've" Challenge:

Challenge yourself to replace "should've, could've, would've" with "learned, can, will" in your self-talk. Instead of dwelling on what you should've done differently, focus on what you've learned and how you can apply those lessons moving forward.

7. Gratitude Rewind:

Rewind the tape of your life and identify moments you regret. Now, find something in each of those moments for which you're grateful. This exercise shifts your perspective from regret to gratitude, emphasising the silver lining in each experience.

Journal prompts:

1. Regret Revue Reflection: Share your experience with the Regret Revue exercise. How did personifying your regrets as characters in a theatrical production impact your perception of them? Did it bring any unexpected insights or humour?

2. Acceptance Time Capsule: Reflect on the process of creating your Acceptance Time Capsule. How did physically burying your regrets symbolise acceptance for you? What emotions or thoughts arose during this exercise?

3. Regret Interview Insights: Summarise the insights gained from the Regret Interview exercise. Did any of your regrets surprise you with their teachings? How did this exercise contribute to your understanding of the lessons embedded in your regrets?

4. Letter to Your Past Self: Share an excerpt from the letter you wrote to your past self. How did writing this letter impact your perspective on a specific regret? Did it evoke any emotions or provide a sense of closure?

5. Regretful Art Therapy Reflection: Describe the art piece you created to express your regrets. How did engaging in artistic expression help you process and release negative energy associated with regret? What emotions or realisations surfaced during this activity?

6. The "Should've, Could've, Would've" Challenge: Share instances where you successfully replaced "should've, could've, would've" with "learned, can, will" in your self-talk.

How did this linguistic shift influence your mindset and approach to past mistakes?

7. Gratitude Rewind Reflection: Reflect on moments in your life that initially sparked regret. How were you able to find gratitude in those experiences? Did this exercise shift your perspective on the role of regret in your personal growth?

Releasing regret is not about erasing the past but transforming it into a source of wisdom and growth. By infusing humour, acceptance, and creativity into the process, you're not just letting go of regrets; you're crafting a narrative of resilience and self-compassion.

The Journey of Self-Compassion: Treating Yourself with Kindness

We're embarking on a profound exploration into the heartwarming realm of self-compassion. Imagine it as a plush, comforting blanket, tailor-made to wrap around your soul, providing a cocoon of warmth without any irritating itchiness. So, grab your metaphorical marshmallows, because we're about to delve into the transformative journey of treating ourselves with the same kindness we generously extend to others.

Self-compassion – more than just a catchy phrase, it's a powerful concept that can revolutionise the way we navigate the complexities of our inner world. If self-love were a spa day, self-compassion would be the VIP treatment, minus the awkward small talk with the massage therapist.

Now, let's unravel the layers of self-compassion, dissecting its essence and understanding why it's not merely a passing trend but a genuine game-changer in the realm of well-being.

At its core, self-compassion is the act of treating oneself with the same kindness, understanding, and forgiveness that we readily offer to our closest friends. It's about being a friend to ourselves in times of struggle, embracing our imperfections, and recognising that we are inherently worthy of love and compassion.

Imagine self-compassion as a sanctuary for the soul, a haven where judgment takes a backseat, and acceptance is the reigning monarch. In a world that often demands perfection and relentless achievement, self-compassion stands as a rebellion – a rebellion against the unrealistic standards we impose on ourselves.

It's important to distinguish self-compassion from self-esteem. While self-esteem often hinges on external validation and accomplishments, self-compassion is an internal, unconditional embrace of oneself, flaws and all. It's not about proclaiming superiority; it's about acknowledging our shared humanity, understanding that everyone faces challenges, makes mistakes, and experiences moments of vulnerability.

So, why is self-compassion a game-changer? Well, imagine navigating the tumultuous seas of life with an unwavering ally within – that's the power of self-compassion. It serves as a lifeboat in moments of self-doubt, a lighthouse in the storm of self-criticism, guiding us towards a harbour of acceptance and kindness.

Now, let's embark on practical exercises that will deepen our understanding of self-compassion and infuse this concept into our daily lives.

1. The Mirror Pep Talk:
Stand in front of a mirror, locking eyes with the incredible individual looking back at you – that's you! Engage in a heartfelt pep talk, showering yourself with the kind of encouragement you'd readily give to a cherished friend. Acknowledge your strengths, celebrate your victories, and throw in a couple of metaphorical fist pumps for good measure. This exercise is not about arrogance; it's about recognising and appreciating the unique qualities that make you, well, you.

2. The Kindness Journal:
Introduce a Kindness Journal into your daily routine. This journal becomes a sacred space where you document moments of self-compassion. Did you cut yourself some slack when things didn't go as planned? Did you treat yourself to a guilty pleasure without the guilt? Celebrate these acts of self-kindness and observe how your self-compassion blossoms with each entry.

3. The "Dear Me" Letter:
Sit down with pen and paper and write a heartfelt letter to yourself, adopting the perspective of your own best friend. What advice would this supportive friend offer you during challenging times? How would they express their unwavering love and

understanding? This exercise is a profound act of self-love, providing comfort and reassurance from the most reliable source – yourself.

4. The Self-Compassion Affirmations:
Craft a set of self-compassion affirmations tailored to your needs and challenges. These affirmations become your arsenal, your verbal shield against the arrows of self-criticism. For example, "I am deserving of love and understanding, especially in moments of difficulty." Revisit and repeat these affirmations regularly, especially during moments of self-doubt or vulnerability.

5. The Comfort Kit:
Assemble a Comfort Kit filled with items that bring you joy and comfort. Whether it's your favourite book, a cozy blanket, or a playlist of feel-good songs, these items become your go-to sources of solace. Whenever you need a boost of self-compassion, indulge in your Comfort Kit, creating a tangible and sensory experience of treating yourself with kindness.

6. The Compliment Challenge:
Challenge yourself to give genuine compliments to yourself every day for a week. This exercise isn't about arrogance or vanity; it's about cultivating a habit of acknowledging your worth. Did you handle a tough situation with grace? Compliment yourself. Did you achieve a personal or professional goal? Shower yourself with praise. By practicing self-compliments, you're fostering a positive and compassionate internal dialogue.

7. The Forgiveness Ritual:
Identify a specific mistake or decision that still lingers in your mind. Create a forgiveness ritual to acknowledge, accept, and release the weight of this experience. It could involve writing the

mistake on a piece of paper, symbolising your commitment to letting it go, and physically disposing of it. This ritual serves as a powerful metaphor for self-compassion – acknowledging our humanity, accepting imperfections, and releasing the burden of past mistakes.

Journal prompts:

1. Mirror Pep Talk Reflection: Share your experience with the Mirror Pep Talk exercise. How did it feel to look yourself in the eyes and offer words of encouragement? Did it bring any emotions or revelations about the way you perceive yourself?

2. Kindness Journal Insights: Reflect on moments you documented in your Kindness Journal. How have acts of self-compassion influenced your mindset and overall well-being? Did you notice any patterns or shifts in your approach to self-kindness?

3. "Dear Me" Letter Excerpt: Share a snippet from the "Dear Me" letter you wrote. What advice did you offer yourself, and how did it feel to express self-love from the perspective of a best friend? Did this exercise evoke any emotions or realisations?

4. Self-Compassion Affirmations: Discuss the self-compassion affirmations you created. How have these affirmations impacted your self-talk and overall mindset? Have you noticed an increase in self-compassion during challenging moments?

5. Comfort Kit Reflection: Describe the items in your Comfort Kit and share how they contribute to your sense of well-being. How does indulging in your Comfort Kit align with the concept of self-compassion? Have you discovered new ways to comfort yourself?

6. Compliment Challenge Achievements: Reflect on your experience with the Compliment Challenge. How did daily self-compliments influence your self-perception? Did it lead to a greater sense of self-compassion?

7. Forgiveness Ritual Insights: Share your experience with the Forgiveness Ritual. How did acknowledging and releasing a past mistake impact your emotional well-being? Did it contribute to a sense of closure or self-forgiveness?

In summary, self-compassion is not a fleeting trend or a mere buzzword; it's a profound and transformative practice that can redefine the way you relate to yourself. By infusing humour, kindness, and acceptance into your daily life through these practical exercises, you're not just engaging in self-care; you're fostering a compassionate and supportive relationship with the most important person in your life – yourself. So, wrap yourself in the plush blanket of self-compassion, savour the warmth it brings, and let the journey of treating yourself with kindness be a perpetual celebration of your inherent worth. You're not just deserving of love and understanding; you're the curator of a boundless reservoir of self-compassion. Here's to embracing the gentle power within you!

Facing Fear Head-On: Transforming Anxiety into Empowerment

We're diving headfirst into the heart of a riveting challenge: confronting anxiety head-on and transmuting it into an unstoppable force for empowerment. Envision this as our superhero training session – no capes required, just a generous serving of humour, a sprinkle of wisdom, and, of course, the strategic deployment of the formidable power of acceptance.

Anxiety – that uninvited guest who stubbornly crashes the party in the vast expanse of our minds. But here's the kicker: we're not allowing it to commandeer the dance floor. Instead, we're orchestrating a spectacular twist, harnessing anxiety as the very fuel that propels our metaphorical jetpacks of empowerment. So, tighten your seatbelts, grab your most comforting blanket (because comfort is the secret ingredient), and join me on this exhilarating journey to transmute anxiety into an unbridled source of empowerment.

Before we plunge into the strategies of empowerment, let's unveil the true nature of our adversary – anxiety. It often disguises itself as a relentless party crasher, disrupting the harmony of our mental space. But what if we could strip away the disguise and expose anxiety for what it truly is – a powerful but manageable force within us?

Humour becomes our trusty sidekick in this battle. Picture it as the Robin to our Batman, lightening the mood and disarming anxiety's potency. By injecting humour into our approach, we gain a fresh perspective, transforming anxiety from a formidable foe into a more manageable companion.

Wisdom, our seasoned mentor, guides us through the intricate dance with anxiety. It whispers insights, helping us navigate the complexities and revealing the hidden pathways to empowerment. Through this strategic alliance of humour and wisdom, we embark on a transformative journey.

Now, let's delve into the heart of our arsenal – the jetpacks of empowerment. And the most crucial element fuelling these jetpacks? Acceptance. It's not about defeating anxiety but accepting its presence and channeling its energy towards our empowerment.

Picture acceptance as the finely tuned engine propelling our jetpacks. It allows us to acknowledge anxiety without succumbing to its overwhelming force. Acceptance is not surrender; it's the art of understanding and navigating the turbulent currents of our emotions.

1. The Fear Flip:
Let's kick things off with a culinary twist – the Fear Flip. Imagine your anxiety as a pancake – not just any pancake, but one brimming with worries and fears. Now, it's time to flip it! Identify that anxiety-inducing fear, and like a seasoned chef flipping pancakes in a dazzling culinary display, reframe it into a positive or empowering statement. It's like turning your fears into a gourmet dish of resilience.

2. Acceptance Affirmations:

Affirmations are like the secret sauce in our empowerment recipe. Develop a set of acceptance affirmations tailored to those anxiety triggers that often sneak up on you. These affirmations are like the secret mantra that whispers, "I accept and embrace, imperfections and all." Repeat them regularly, especially when anxiety comes knocking, and watch how they become the antidote to anxious thoughts.

3. Fear Journaling:

Picture your thoughts as intrepid explorers in the vast wilderness of your mind. Start a Fear Journal where these explorers document the anxious terrains they encounter. But here's the plot twist — after noting down the fear, challenge it with a counterargument. It's like sending your thoughts on a daring expedition, arming them with logic and reasoning against the irrational fears that lurk in the shadows.

4. The Comfort Challenge:

It's time to level up — identify a situation that triggers anxiety but is manageable. Think of it as the training ground for your superhero skills. Start small, expose yourself gradually, and watch as your comfort zone expands like a superhero in action. This exercise is like a superhero workout for your resilience muscles, turning anxiety into a stepping stone for personal growth.

5. Anxiety Avatar:

Picture this: your anxiety transformed into a quirky character, a sidekick or a mischievous imp. By giving anxiety a face and personality, you're externalising it — turning it into a whimsical companion instead of a looming threat. Draw or describe your anxiety avatar, and when anxiety shows up, imagine it doing a little dance in the background. It's like turning anxiety into your weird but lovable sidekick.

6. Radical Acceptance:
We're diving deep into the superhero lore with the concept of radical acceptance. This means acknowledging and accepting things as they are, without judgment or resistance. When anxiety strikes, instead of going into battle mode, practice radical acceptance. It's like telling anxiety, "Hey, I see you, and I'm not letting you hijack the narrative. I've got this."

7. Empowerment Playlist:
Every superhero needs a theme song, right? Create an Empowerment Playlist filled with tunes that make you feel like you can conquer the world. When anxiety creeps in, cue your personal soundtrack and let the music transform your mental landscape. It's like having a superhero anthem for every battle against fears.

Journal prompts:

1. Fear Flip Reflection: Share your experience with the Fear Flip exercise. How did reframing your fear into a positive statement impact your perspective? Did it feel like you were turning the tables on anxiety, making it work for you instead of against you?

2. Acceptance Affirmations: Discuss the acceptance affirmations you developed. How do these affirmations resonate with your anxiety triggers? Have they become like a soothing melody in the background, countering the cacophony of anxious thoughts?

3. *Fear Journaling Insights:* Reflect on your Fear Journal entries. How did challenging your anxious thoughts with counterarguments affect your perception of the fears? Did it feel like you were leading a mental expedition against the irrational fears that often lurk in the shadows?

4. *The Comfort Challenge Experience:* Share your journey with the Comfort Challenge. How did gradually exposing yourself to anxiety-inducing situations impact your tolerance and resilience? Did it feel like you were levelling up your superhero skills, turning anxiety into a stepping stone for personal growth?

5. *Anxiety Avatar Description:* Describe your anxiety avatar – the quirky character representing your anxiety. How does personifying anxiety help externalise it? Did it make anxiety feel less overwhelming or intimidating? Share any creative insights from this exercise.

6. *Radical Acceptance Reflection:* Discuss your experience with practicing radical acceptance. How did acknowledging and accepting things as they are influence your response to anxiety? Did it feel like you were disarming anxiety by embracing it with an open heart?

7. *Empowerment Playlist Highlights:* Share the songs from your Empowerment Playlist and how they make you feel. How does music contribute to your sense of empowerment and strength? Did it feel like your personal soundtrack for every battle against fears?

Transforming anxiety into empowerment is not about erasing fear; it's about reshaping its role in your narrative. By infusing humour, acceptance, and practical exercises into the process, you're not just facing fears; you're becoming the superhero of your own story. So, embrace your anxiety, turn it into a trusty sidekick, and let the journey from fear to empowerment be a celebration of your indomitable spirit. Remember, you're not defined by your anxiety; you're empowered by your ability to face it head-on!

Mind-Body Harmony: Understanding the Interconnectedness of Well-being

Grab your favourite comfy blanket and get cozy because we're about to unlock the secrets to revitalising your life.

So, you've probably heard about the mind-body connection, right? It's not some mystical concept or a secret society's password; it's the real deal. Our minds and bodies are like two dance partners, and when they groove together, that's when the magic happens.

Let's start with a little exercise – don't worry; I promise it won't involve extreme yoga poses or chanting mantras (unless you're into that, then by all means, go for it).

1. The Power of Mindful Breathing:
Find a quiet spot where you won't be disturbed. Sit comfortably, close your eyes, and take a deep breath in. Feel the air filling your lungs, and then exhale slowly. Repeat this for a few minutes, focusing only on your breath.
As you do this, let go of any tension or stress. Imagine your worries floating away with each exhale. It's like a mini-vacation for your mind.

Now, let's talk about how our thoughts can sometimes be like a chaotic monkey party in our minds. We've got this constant chatter, questioning, and self-doubt that can be utterly exhausting. But fear not, my friends, because the power of acceptance is about to swoop in like a superhero.

2. Embracing the Monkey Mind:
Picture your mind as a room full of mischievous monkeys. They're swinging from the chandeliers, tossing banana peels everywhere – chaos, right? Instead of trying to shush them, accept the monkey madness. Acknowledge the thoughts without judgment, like you're watching a quirky sitcom. It's your mind's own sitcom, starring you!
Acceptance doesn't mean giving in to negative thoughts; it means understanding that they're part of the show. The more you accept, the less power those monkeys have over you.

Now, let's add some laughter into the mix. Laughter is like a secret ingredient in the recipe for a happy, harmonious life. It's not just about telling jokes; it's about finding joy in the little absurdities of life.

3. Laughter Yoga:
Yes, it's a real thing! Stand or sit comfortably, and start with some hearty laughter, even if it feels forced at first. Laugh like nobody's watching (or like everyone is – embrace the absurdity!). Keep going, and soon, genuine laughter will bubble up. It's contagious, and trust me, your body will thank you for this burst of positivity.

Let's talk about the undeniable connection between our physical well-being and our mental state. Remember, it's not about looking like a fitness model; it's about finding activities that make you feel good inside and out.

4. Joyful Movement:
Think about an activity that brings you genuine joy – whether it's dancing like no one's watching, walking in nature, or even hula-hooping in your living room. Commit to doing this activity regularly, not as a chore but as a celebration of what your body can do. The key is joy, not judgment.

Acceptance doesn't mean resignation; it means recognising your body's uniqueness and working with it, not against it. Now, let's spice things up with some more acceptance goodness.

5. Acceptance Exercise: Mirror Affirmations:
Stand in front of a mirror and look yourself in the eyes. Repeat positive affirmations about your body and yourself. Embrace the

imperfections and celebrate the journey your body has taken you on. It's not about perfection; it's about progress and self-love.

As we wrap up our mind-body harmony session, remember that acceptance is your golden ticket to reclaiming vitality. It's not a one-time thing but a continuous, compassionate practice. So, let's sprinkle a bit of humour, a dash of mindfulness, and a whole lot of acceptance into our daily lives.

Journal Prompts:

1. Reflect on the laughter yoga exercise. What surprised you about the experience, and how did it make you feel?

2. Explore the concept of accepting your thoughts as mischievous monkeys. How can you apply this acceptance to your daily life?

3. Describe the joyful movement activity you chose. How does it make you feel, and how can you incorporate it into your routine regularly?

4. Share your experience with mirror affirmations. What positive affirmations resonated with you, and how can you continue embracing self-love through this practice?

Remember, my tired, not lazy friends, you're on a journey of rediscovery. Embrace the harmony between your mind and body, and watch as the symphony of vitality plays on. Keep embracing the chaos, finding joy in the absurd, and accepting the wonderfully unique masterpiece that is you!

Balancing Act: Navigating the Challenges of Work and Life

We're diving into the circus act known as balancing work and life. It's not about becoming a master tightrope walker. It's about accepting that sometimes, you might drop a few balls, and that's perfectly okay.

Let's start with a reality check – work can be demanding. Whether you're hustling in the corporate world or juggling kids at home, finding that elusive work-life balance can feel like searching for a unicorn. But fear not, my friends, because we're about to turn this balancing act into a comedy show. Get ready for some practical exercises that will have you laughing your way through the chaos.

1. The Work-Life To-Do List:
Grab a pen and paper (or your preferred digital device) and make two columns. On one side, list your work-related to-dos, and on the other, jot down your personal tasks. Now, take a step back

and look at your list. Is it longer than a CVS receipt? Yeah, mine too.

Acceptance isn't about magically making your to-do list disappear. It's about embracing the chaos and acknowledging that you're a superhero, but even superheroes have limits. Identify three tasks from each column that are non-negotiable and can't be delegated. The rest? Well, those are negotiable. It's not about doing it all but doing what matters most.

2. The 'No' Comedy Challenge:
Raise your hand if you're a people pleaser. I see you! Now, here's the challenge: for one week, say 'no' to at least one non-essential request or commitment with a comedic twist. Channel your inner stand-up comedian and make it light-hearted. For example, "Sorry, I can't join your pottery class, I've got a secret mission to find my lost socks."

The key here is not just saying 'no' but doing it with a smile and a sprinkle of humour. It's a game-changer, trust me.

3. The Imperfectly Balanced Scale:
Imagine your life as a balancing scale. On one side, you've got work, and on the other, you've got personal life. The goal isn't to make both sides perfectly even. Instead, accept that some days work might weigh a bit heavier, and other days, your personal life takes the lead.

Embrace the imbalance as a natural part of the dance between work and life. It's not about perfection; it's about finding the rhythm that works for you. Oh, and don't forget to add a funky dance move to that scale. Life's too short for boring balancing acts!

4. The Multitasking Circus:

Create a multitasking challenge for yourself. Pick three tasks that you usually do separately and try doing them simultaneously. Picture this: answering emails while doing squats or folding laundry while brainstorming your next brilliant idea. The goal here isn't perfection – it's embracing the chaos with a smile.

Accept that multitasking doesn't mean flawlessly executing every task simultaneously. It means finding the hilarity in the juggling act and celebrating the small victories, even if they involve mismatched socks or a slightly wrinkled shirt.

5. The Mindful Minute:

Set a timer for one minute and close your eyes. Take a deep breath in, hold it for a moment, and then exhale slowly. During this minute, let go of the chaos and focus on the present moment. Accept that, in this minute, you don't have to be the superhero or the circus performer. You can just be you.

Inhale the acceptance, exhale the expectations. It's a brief but powerful reset that can help you navigate the challenges of your personal circus with a newfound sense of calm.

As we wrap up our balancing act session, remember that acceptance is the tightrope walker's safety net. It's not about avoiding falls but learning to bounce back with style.

Journal Prompts:

1. Reflect on your experience with the 'No' Comedy Challenge. How did adding humour to saying 'no' affect your mindset and the reactions of others?

2. Explore the concept of the Imperfectly Balanced Scale. How can you embrace the natural ebb and flow between work and personal life without striving for perfection?

3. Share your multitasking circus experience. What tasks did you choose, and how did embracing the chaos with a smile impact your approach to those tasks?

4. Write about your Mindful Minute. How did taking a brief moment for mindfulness contribute to your sense of acceptance and calm during a busy day?

Remember, my fellow jugglers of life, the circus might be chaotic, but it's also filled with laughter, surprises, and a whole lot of acceptance. So, toss those juggling balls high, embrace the imperfections, and let the show go on!

Resilience in Adversity: Finding Strength in Life's Tests

We're strapping ourselves in for an exploration of the fine art of bouncing back, giving adversity the side-eye, and discovering the superhero strength within us when faced with life's most unexpected pop quizzes.

Life's not a leisurely stroll in a well-manicured park; it's more like stumbling through a twisted scavenger hunt in the pitch-black darkness with a flashlight that's decided to play hide-and-seek. But, fear not, because it's precisely in this darkness that we find our inner glow-sticks – our resilience. So, buckle up, because we're about to embark on a journey filled with practical exercises that will have you flexing your resilience muscles like never before.

Before we dive into the exercises, let's take a moment to appreciate the significance of resilience. Imagine yourself as a glow-stick – that bendable, light-emitting wonder. Life, with its unexpected twists and turns, is like the force that bends and shakes you. Resilience is your ability to glow brightly even in the midst of that bending and shaking.

So, here's the deal: life will throw challenges your way. It's not a matter of 'if' but 'when.' Resilience is your secret weapon, your inner glow-stick that lights up the darkness. Now, let's equip ourselves with some practical tools to harness that glows tick power.

1. The Bounce-Back Playlist:

Music, my friends, has this magical ability to lift us up, shake off the dust, and make us want to dance through the storm. Your task: create the ultimate Bounce-Back Playlist. These are not just any songs; they're your personal anthems of resilience. The ones that make you want to conquer the world, or at the very least, conquer the challenges of the day.

When life throws a curveball your way, hit play on your Bounce-Back Playlist. Let the beats be the rhythm of your comeback story. Acceptance here doesn't mean pretending everything is fine; it means acknowledging the challenge and choosing to respond with a dance move rather than a defeated slump. Remember, even Beyoncé has bad days; it's all about how she bounces back.

2. The Comedy Roast:

Our inner dialogue can be a real drama queen, turning a minor setback into an Oscar-worthy catastrophe. Time to dim the spotlight on that drama and bring in the laughter. Enter the Comedy Roast.

Imagine your negative thoughts as stand-up comedians performing a roast about your life. Get creative – give them ridiculous names like Debbie Downer or Pessimism Pete. Now, play the mental scenario of a comedy roast where they throw their best insults your way.

The twist? Respond with humour. Picture yourself as the confident host, deflecting their negativity with witty comebacks. It's not about ignoring the challenges; it's about roasting them into submission with a smile.

Acceptance is about acknowledging the negative thoughts without letting them dictate the narrative of your life. So, let the comedy roast begin!

3. The Perspective Flip:
Life's tests often come with multiple-choice questions, and our perspective is the answer key. Time to choose the perspective that turns adversity into a plot twist rather than a tragic tale.
Identify a recent challenge and write down the negative thoughts associated with it. Now, flip the perspective by finding at least three positive or humorous angles. For example, "I didn't get the promotion" becomes "I've just been promoted to Chief Office Snack Coordinator."

It's not about downplaying the difficulty; it's about choosing a perspective that empowers rather than disheartens. Acceptance, in this context, means embracing the challenge with a mindset that turns setbacks into setups for future success.

4. The Resilience Squad:
Batman needs Alfred, and peanut butter needs jelly. Similarly, we all need someone in our corner during tough times. Enter your Resilience Squad.
Identify three people in your life who lift you up, make you laugh, or provide a comforting ear when needed. Share with them the concept of being your 'Resilience Squad.' Let them know you appreciate their support and, in turn, offer to be part of their squad.

Acceptance in relationships is about opening up, sharing vulnerabilities, and building a network of support. Your Resilience Squad is there not to fix everything but to remind you that you're not facing life's tests alone.

5. The Comedy Journal:

Laughter is a healing potion for the soul, and your Comedy Journal is the Hogwarts of resilience. Start jotting down funny observations, silly moments, or humorous thoughts daily. When facing adversity, revisit your Comedy Journal.

Acceptance in this exercise is about finding joy even in the midst of challenges, recognising that laughter is a powerful tool for resilience.

As we wrap up our resilience boot camp, remember that adversity is the unexpected plot twist in the novel of life. You're not the victim; you're the badass protagonist navigating the unpredictable storyline.

Journal Prompts:

1. Reflect on your experience with the Bounce-Back Playlist. Which songs resonated with you the most, and how did they impact your mood when facing a challenge?

2. Explore the Comedy Roast exercise. What creative names did you give to your negative thoughts, and how did responding with humour shift your perspective?

3. Share your Perspective Flip exercise. How did turning a negative situation into a positive or humorous one impact your mindset and resilience?

4. Write about your Resilience Squad. Who are the three people you identified, and how can you strengthen these connections to build a robust support system?

5. Revisit your Comedy Journal. Share a few entries that brought a smile to your face during challenging times. How does humour contribute to your resilience and overall well-being?

Life's tests may be tough, but so are you. Embrace the challenges, dance through the chaos, and remember that your resilience is a force to be reckoned with.

The Power of Saying "No": Setting Healthy Boundaries

We navigate the exhilarating terrain of setting healthy boundaries – a skill that's as crucial as knowing your coffee order by heart. Let's dive into the art of saying "No" without feeling like a party pooper and embrace the liberating magic that comes with it.

Now, picture this: you're a zen master in the grand cinematic universe of your life. But even zen masters need to know when to set up their tranquil space. It's time to equip yourself with the superpower of setting boundaries – a skill that will make a monk's meditation cushion look like child's play.

Before we unleash our boundary-setting prowess, let's debunk the myth that saying "No" makes you a joy-killing villain. Nope, not true. In fact, saying "No" is like flexing your inner zen muscle; it's a declaration of self-respect and a commitment to preserving your peace.

Now, onto the practical exercises that will turn you into the boundary-setting zen master you were always meant to be.

1. The Boundary Inventory:
Grab a notebook, and let's do a little inventory. List three recent instances where you wish you had said "No." Maybe it was agreeing to an extra project at work or attending yet another virtual event. Reflect on how these situations made you feel. Was it stress, overwhelm, or a tinge of regret?

Acceptance is the first step here – acknowledging that these moments happened, and they had an impact on your well-being. Now, let's gear up for the zen transformation.

2. The Empowerment Playlist:
Create an Empowerment Playlist – songs that make you feel strong, confident, and ready to conquer the world. When you're gearing up to say "No," press play on this playlist. Channel your inner zen master as you approach those boundary-setting moments.

Recognise that setting boundaries doesn't make you a bad person. It makes you the lead meditator in the sanctuary of your own life, hitting those high notes of self-respect.

3. The Kind No:
Now, let's practice the "Kind No." Saying "No" doesn't have to be a cold, heartless rejection. It can be a warm, empathetic

response that preserves your boundaries while showing respect for others.

Imagine a friend asks for a favour that you genuinely can't manage. Instead of a blunt "No," try saying, "I appreciate you thinking of me, but unfortunately, I won't be able to help with that right now." The key here is maintaining your boundaries without burning bridges.

Your time and energy are valuable, and it's okay to protect them.

4. The Yes to Yourself Jar:
Create a "Yes to Yourself Jar." Decorate a jar and every time you say "No" to something that aligns with your boundaries, jot it down on a piece of paper and throw it into the jar. Celebrate these victories – they're evidence of your commitment to self-care and well-being.

Embrace the idea that saying "No" to others often means saying "Yes" to yourself – a powerful act of self-love.

5. The Boundary-Setting Dialogue:
Practice a boundary-setting dialogue with a friend or even in front of the mirror. Imagine a scenario where you need to decline an invitation or set a limit at work. Practice saying your "No" with a firm yet polite tone. It's not about rehearsing to be robotic; it's about finding your authentic voice.

Your needs are valid, and expressing them doesn't make you selfish – it makes you human.

6. The Declutter Challenge:

Think of your life as a room filled with stuff. Some things bring you joy, while others are just clutter. Decluttering is about making space for what matters. Apply this to your schedule – identify one commitment that doesn't align with your priorities and gracefully decline it.

Acknowledge that a simplified life is a more fulfilling life. It's about curating your time and energy like a zen master.

Now, let's sprinkle in some humour to lighten the boundary-setting mood.

7. The Hilarious "No" Rejection Lines:

Come up with a list of hilarious "No" rejection lines. Picture this: someone asks you to do something you just can't commit to, and you respond with a funny yet clear rejection. For example, "I'd love to, but my pet rock has a spa day that day, and I promised to be the chauffeur."

Humour can be a fantastic tool for setting boundaries without being confrontational.

Journal Prompts:

1. Reflect on your Boundary Inventory. How did those instances make you feel, and what impact did they have on your well-being?

2. Share a few songs from your Empowerment Playlist. How do these songs make you feel, and how can they empower you to set boundaries?

3. Practice the "Kind No" in a real-life scenario. How did it feel to communicate your boundaries with warmth and empathy?

4. Write about your "Yes to Yourself Jar" victories. How does celebrating these moments contribute to your sense of

self-love and well-being?

5. Explore the Boundary-Setting Dialogue exercise. How did practicing your "No" help you find your authentic voice in expressing your needs?

6. Share a rejection line from your Hilarious "No" Rejection Lines list. How can humour be a tool for setting boundaries in a lighthearted way?

Saying "No" is not a rejection of others; it's a declaration of self-respect. So, put on your zen master robes, embrace the power of your "No," and let the world know that your boundaries are non-negotiable.

Letting Go of Toxic Influences: Creating Space for Positivity

Hey fabulous readers! It's Emily, your go-to life enthusiast, back to chat about the magical act of clearing out the negativity cluttering our lives. We're delving into the art of letting go of toxic influences – a skill more crucial than successfully executing a ninja-level parallel parking manoeuvre. Get ready to make space for the good vibes and bid adieu to the energy vampires in your life.

Now, envision this: you're the curator of a high-end art gallery, and your life is the exhibit. It's time to declutter those toxic paintings and sculptures that zap your positive energy. Let's get rid of the drama-filled abstracts and make room for the serene landscapes of positivity.

Before we start tossing out the negativity like confetti, let's understand what we mean by toxic influences. These are the energy vampires, the joy-stealers, and the drama llamas that leave you emotionally drained faster than a juice cleanse. Acceptance, in this context, is about recognising these influences without judgment – no blame game, just a Marie Kondo-inspired evaluation of what sparks joy in your life.

Now, let's plunge into some practical exercises that'll make you a pro at energetic Marie Kondo-ing.

1. The Toxic Tally:
Grab a notepad, and let's do a toxic tally. List down the people, situations, or habits in your life that leave you feeling more drained than a smartphone on 1% battery. Be honest with yourself – this is a judgment-free zone.

Acceptance is the first step here – acknowledging that these influences exist and understanding their impact on your overall well-being.

2. The Positivity Vision Board:
Create a Positivity Vision Board. Gather magazines, scissors, and a big board. Cut out images and phrases that represent positivity, joy, and well-being. Stick them on your board and place it somewhere visible. This visual reminder will be your daily dose of inspiration to counteract the negativity.

Positivity is not just a fleeting emotion but a lifestyle choice. Your Positivity Vision Board is the visual manifestation of that choice.

3. The Energising Unfollow Spree:
Time to unleash the mighty power of the 'Unfollow' button! Scroll through your social media and identify accounts that consistently bring negativity into your feed. Unfollow them with the swift precision of a ninja warrior. Your social media space should be a sanctuary, not a battleground.
Curating your online environment is a form of self-love and self-care.

4. The Toxic-Free Zone Declaration:
Declare certain spaces in your life as Toxic-Free Zones. It could be your bedroom, your workspace, or even your favourite reading

nook. Fill these spaces with positivity – plants, uplifting quotes, or anything that brings you joy. Make it a rule: no negativity allowed in these designated areas.

Acknowledge that you have the power to create spaces that nurture your well-being.

5. The Positive People Inventory:
Make a list of positive people in your life – those who lift you up, support you, and bring joy to your world. Reflect on how you can spend more time with these individuals. It's not about cutting off everyone; it's about consciously choosing who you surround yourself with.
It's okay to prioritise relationships that contribute positively to your life.

6. The Toxic Habit Swap:
Identify a toxic habit that contributes to negativity in your life. It could be excessive screen time, procrastination, or negative self-talk. Replace this habit with a positive one. For instance, swap mindless scrolling with a short mindfulness meditation or replace negative thoughts with affirmations.

Change is a gradual process, and small positive habits can lead to significant shifts.

7. The Laughter Cleanse:
Engage in a laughter cleanse. Watch a funny movie, attend a stand-up comedy show, or engage in any activity that makes you laugh until your abs hurt. Laughter is a potent antidote to negativity, and it's a fun way to reset your energy.
Finding joy in the midst of challenges is not only permissible but necessary.

Journal Prompts:

1. Reflect on your Toxic Tally. How did it feel to acknowledge the influences that drain your energy, and what insights did you gain from this exercise?

2. Share a few elements from your Positivity Vision Board. How do these images and phrases resonate with your vision of a positive and joyful life?

3. Write about your experience with the Energising Unfollow Spree. How did curating your online space impact your overall mood and well-being?

4. Describe your designated Toxic-Free Zone. What positive elements did you introduce, and how does this space contribute to your daily life?

5. Reflect on your Positive People Inventory. How can you intentionally nurture relationships with those who bring positivity into your life?

6. Share your experience with the Toxic Habit Swap. How did replacing a negative habit with a positive one impact your daily routine and mindset?

7. Write about your Laughter Cleanse. What activity did you choose, and how did it contribute to resetting your energy and creating a more positive outlook?

Remember, letting go of toxic influences is not about being harsh or judgmental; it's about creating space for positivity and joy. So, put on your curator hat, declutter that negative art, and let the vibrant hues of positivity take centre stage in the gallery of your life.

Embracing Aging: Finding the Wisdom in Growing Older

Ready to dive into the fountain of youth, metaphorically speaking? Now, we're talking about the fine art of embracing the inevitable – aging. So, grab your reading glasses and let's explore how we can fully welcome the wisdom that comes with growing older without spiralling into a midlife crisis.

Now, picture this: you're a fine wine, getting better with age, or maybe a cheese – aged to perfection, of course. Aging is not the enemy; it's the secret sauce that adds flavour to the recipe of life. Let's sprinkle some humour into this aging journey and uncover the joy in the wrinkles and the wisdom in the grey hairs.

Before we start applauding our laugh lines and giving a standing ovation to our silver strands, let's debunk the myth that aging is synonymous with doom and gloom. Here, it's not just about surrendering to gravity's pull but acknowledging that each passing year is another chapter in our life's comedy show, complete with unexpected punchlines and well-earned wisdom.

Now, onto the practical exercises that will have you aging like a fine Bordeaux.

1. The Mirror Pep Talk:
Stand in front of the mirror and give yourself a Mirror Pep Talk. Compliment the lines that tell the stories of your laughter, the grey hairs that scream wisdom, and the undeniable charm that comes with the passing years. It's not about denying the aging process; it's about celebrating the journey.
Your reflection is a map of the incredible adventures you've navigated.

2. The Time Capsule Letter:
Write a letter to your future self. Pour your current wisdom, dreams, and quirks onto paper. Seal it in an envelope and put it in a safe place. Open it on your next birthday or a significant milestone. This exercise is a reminder that, just like fine wine, you're evolving and getting better with time.
Each year is an opportunity for growth, learning, and creating a legacy.

3. The Nostalgia Night:
Pick a night to indulge in a Nostalgia Night. Watch movies, listen to music, or flip through photo albums that take you back to the good old days. It's not about longing for the past but appreciating the richness of your life's journey.
Every era of your life has contributed to the masterpiece that is you.

4. The Age-Positive Affirmations:

Create a list of Age-Positive Affirmations. These are not just feel-good phrases; they're empowering statements that celebrate the beauty in aging. Repeat them daily. For example, "With age comes wisdom, and I am a beacon of knowledge," or "I embrace the changes in my body as a testament to a life well-lived."

Affirmations are not about denying reality but reframing it with a positive perspective.

5. The Bucket List Boogie:

Dance your way through a Bucket List Boogie. Write down experiences, big or small, that you want to have in the coming years. It could be learning a new language, traveling to a dream destination, or mastering a dance move. Age is just a number; the bucket list is your invitation to live fully.
Life's adventures don't come with an expiry date.

6. The Gratitude Journal for Aging:

Start a Gratitude Journal specifically for aging. Each day, jot down something about the aging process that you're grateful for. It could be the wisdom gained, the relationships formed, or the newfound appreciation for simple pleasures. Aging is not the enemy; it's a privilege denied to many.
Gratitude is a powerful tool for shifting perspective.

7. The Anti-Gravity Yoga:

Engage in some Anti-Gravity Yoga – not the kind where you're suspended in mid-air but the type where you defy the societal pressures to look a certain way as you age. Let go of the societal expectations and embrace the freedom to be authentically you.

The real fountain of youth lies in authenticity.

Journal Prompts:

1. Reflect on your Mirror Pep Talk. How did it feel to celebrate the visible signs of aging, and what positive affirmations did you embrace?

2. Share your experience with the Time Capsule Letter. What insights did you gain from writing to your future self, and how has it shifted your perspective on aging?

3. Write about your Nostalgia Night. What memories did you revisit, and how did it contribute to your appreciation of your life's journey?

4. Explore your Age-Positive Affirmations. Which affirmations resonate with you the most, and how can you incorporate them into your daily routine?

5. Share your Bucket List Boogie. What experiences do you want to embrace in the coming years, and how does this shift your mindset about aging?

6. Write about your Gratitude Journal for Aging. What aspects of the aging process are you grateful for, and how has this practice influenced your outlook on growing older?

7. Reflect on the Anti-Gravity Yoga exercise. How did it feel to let go of societal expectations and embrace the freedom to age authentically?

Remember, my aging-but-still-breathtaking comrades, embracing the wisdom in growing older is not about fighting the clock but dancing to your own rhythm. So, put on those reading glasses, throw some glitter on those laugh lines, allow the world to behold the masterpiece that is your existence, aging like a fine work of art.

Self-Care Rituals: Nurturing Your Mind, Body, and Soul

Let's embark on a journey into the enchanting world of self-care rituals – those meticulously designed nuggets of joy that serve to rejuvenate your mind, pamper your body, and cradle your soul in a comforting embrace.

Imagine, if you will, that you are not just a mere mortal navigating life's twists and turns. No, you are the undisputed star of your very own wellness epic, and the scenes that steal the spotlight are your daily self-care rituals. These aren't just indulgences; they are the blockbuster moments that leave you feeling like the protagonist of a Hollywood sensation. Self-care, contrary to some misconceptions, isn't a frivolous luxury; it's as indispensable as Wi-Fi or that comforting bar of chocolate.

Before we plunge headlong into the labyrinth of self-care, let's dispel a lingering myth that often associates it solely with extravagant spa days or jet-setting off to exotic locales like Bali for solo soul-searching. Self-care, in its purest essence, is the delicate art of embracing and nurturing your unique being. It's an intimate acknowledgement that your well-being isn't a mere afterthought but a non-negotiable priority, a vital component of your journey through this extraordinary tapestry of life.

Now, let's explore the concept of self-care as not just a collection of activities but a profound philosophy that underscores the inherent value within you. Think of it as a deliberate act of self-recognition, acknowledging your worthiness to receive the care and attention you so readily extend to others.

In a world that often glorifies the hustle, the relentless pursuit of goals, and the constant comparison to external standards, self-care emerges as the counter-narrative – a gentle yet powerful reminder that taking time for yourself is not a selfish act but a fundamental aspect of a fulfilling life.

So, as we embark on this exploration, envision your self-care journey as a sacred pact with yourself – a commitment to honour your physical, emotional, and spiritual well-being. It transcends the superficial and delves deep into the core of who you are, embracing your strengths, quirks, and vulnerabilities.

To navigate the self-care odyssey effectively, it's imperative to redefine the concept, stripping away any preconceived notions of extravagance or impracticality. Self-care is an evolving practice that adapts to your unique needs and circumstances.

Begin by acknowledging that self-care isn't a one-size-fits-all solution. It's not about conforming to societal expectations or emulating Instagram-perfect versions of self-love. Instead, it's about crafting a bespoke self-care routine tailored to your preferences, allowing you the freedom to choose activities that genuinely resonate with your soul.

Think of self-care rituals not as mere checkboxes on a to-do list but as intentional moments of presence and mindfulness. These rituals could range from a morning meditation to a leisurely afternoon stroll, from indulging in your favourite book to savouring a cup of tea in solitude. The key is to approach these moments with a sense of reverence and authenticity.

Let's address the misconception that self-care is a privilege reserved for those with an abundance of time or resources. In reality, self-care is an accessible and inclusive practice that can be woven into the fabric of your everyday life. It's about finding joy in the small, mundane moments and prioritising your well-being even amid life's inevitable challenges.

As we traverse this landscape of self-care, consider it not as a temporary escape but as an ongoing investment in your overall wellness. It's about cultivating a sustainable self-care lifestyle that fortifies you against the ebbs and flows of life, enhancing your resilience and capacity to navigate challenges with grace.

Now that we've laid the groundwork for understanding self-care as a philosophy and not just a set of activities, let's translate these insights into actionable steps. Remember, the goal is not perfection but a genuine and compassionate commitment to your well-being.

1. The Guilt-Free Yes:

Practice the "Guilt-Free Yes." Say "yes" to something that brings you joy without a hint of guilt. Whether it's indulging in your favourite dessert, binge-watching guilty pleasure TV, or taking a spontaneous day off, allow yourself the pleasure of saying "yes" without the usual mental baggage.

Self-care is not selfish; it's an act of self-love.

2. The Mindful Munch:

Engage in the Mindful Munch. Pick a favourite snack and savour each bite. Pay attention to the textures, flavours, and sensations. This exercise is not about restricting yourself; it's about savouring the simple joys without the distraction of screens or to-do lists.

Self-care can start with small, mindful moments in your daily routine.

3. The Hug-a-Day Challenge:

Embark on the Hug-a-Day Challenge. Hug yourself for a minimum of 10 seconds every day. It might feel a bit silly at first, but soon you'll realise the power of self-compassion. Bonus points if you add a self-affirmation during the embrace.

Self-love is a daily practice that starts with a simple hug.

4. The Tech Detox Fiesta:

Host a Tech Detox Fiesta. Dedicate an evening to disconnecting from screens and digital distractions. Engage in activities that bring you joy without the glow of electronic devices. It's not about demonising technology but creating space for analog pleasures.

Understanding in the Tech Detox Fiesta is recognising the impact of digital detox on mental well-being.

5. The Joyful Movement Break:
Introduce a Joyful Movement Break into your routine. It doesn't have to be a rigorous workout; it could be a dance party in your living room, a stroll in the park, or a gentle yoga session. The key is to move your body in a way that brings you joy.

Movement is a celebration of what your body can do, not a punishment for what you ate.

6. The Gratitude Giggles Journal:
Start a Gratitude Giggles Journal. Each day, jot down something that made you laugh or brought a smile to your face. It could be a funny moment, a joke, or even a hilarious meme. Laughter is a powerful self-care tool.

Humour is a vital aspect of self-care that shouldn't be underestimated.

7. The Spa Day at Home:
Host a Spa Day at Home, but add a humorous twist. Imagine you're a character in a comedy movie – wear a face mask and cucumbers on your eyes while reciting your favourite jokes or funny movie quotes. The key is to indulge in self-care with a side of laughter.

Self-care can be both nurturing and hilarious.

Journal Prompts:

1. Reflect on your Guilt-Free Yes experience. How did it feel to say "yes" without guilt, and what insights did you gain about prioritising your joy?

2. Share your Mindful Munch observations. How did savouring a snack mindfully impact your overall well-being, and what small joys did you discover?

3. Write about your Hug-a-Day Challenge. How did daily self-hugging influence your sense of self-compassion, and did you incorporate self-affirmations during the hugs?

4. Reflect on your Tech Detox Fiesta. How did disconnecting from screens enhance your analog pleasures, and what realisations did you have during this tech-free time?

5. Explore your Joyful Movement Break. What form of joyful movement did you engage in, and how did it contribute to a positive relationship with your body?

6. Write about your Gratitude Giggles Journal. How did incorporating humour into your gratitude practice impact your daily outlook and overall well-being?

7. Share your Spa Day at Home with a humorous twist. How did combining self-care with laughter enhance the experience, and what funny moments did you create?

Self-care is not a luxury; it's a celebration of your existence. So, grab your self-love toolkit, dive into these delightful exercises, and let the laughter-filled self-care rituals be the daily blockbuster that is your life.

Shifting Focus to the Bright Side of Life

We're diving deep into the art of gratitude journaling – a practice that's like a daily dose of glitter for your soul. So, grab your favourite pen, find a cozy nook, and let's sprinkle some gratitude magic into our lives!

Now, let's kick things off by acknowledging that life can be a wild rollercoaster, complete with unexpected loop-de-loops and the occasional stomach drop. But don't worry! Gratitude journaling is our secret weapon, our compass guiding us to the bright side, even when the ride gets a bit too crazy.

Let's break down any preconceived notions. It's not about writing Shakespearean sonnets or composing epic novels of appreciation. No need for fancy words or profound thoughts. Gratitude journaling is like a casual chat with your best friend, where you spill the beans on the fantastic things happening in your life.

Picture this: You're not just journaling; you're creating a glittering trail of positivity. Gratitude is your wand, and each entry is a sprinkle of magic dust, turning the ordinary into extraordinary.

1. The Daily Delight List:
Let's kick off our gratitude adventure with the Daily Delight List. Every day, jot down three things that brought a smile to your face. It could be anything – from the neighbour's goofy wave to finding a forgotten chocolate bar in your pantry. No matter how small or seemingly insignificant, embrace the joy.

Happiness often resides in the little moments, waiting to be noticed.

2. The Marvellous Mishaps Chronicle:
Now, let's flip the script with the Marvellous Mishaps Chronicle. Recall a recent blunder or mishap and find the silver lining. Did you spill coffee on your favourite shirt? Well, it's now a custom-designed coffee art piece! Turning mishaps into marvels is an art, my friends.
Even in chaos, there's room for gratitude and a good laugh.

3. The "Unexpected Kindness" Scavenger Hunt:
Embark on the "Unexpected Kindness" Scavenger Hunt. Throughout the day, keep an eye out for unexpected acts of kindness, whether big or small. It could be a stranger holding the door, a colleague offering help, or a friend sending a random uplifting message. Document these moments in your journal.
Kindness surrounds us, often where we least expect it.

4. The Past-Present-Future Love Letter:
Get a little mushy with the Past-Present-Future Love Letter. Write a letter expressing gratitude for something in your past, celebrating a joyous moment in your present, and expressing excitement for a future experience. It's a triple-layered gratitude cake!
Gratitude extends across the timeline of our lives.

5. The "Aha!" Reflections:
Engage in the "Aha!" Reflections. Take a moment to reflect on a recent realisation or insight. It could be a personal revelation, a newfound skill, or simply seeing a situation from a different

perspective. Gratitude isn't just about things; it's about the wisdom gained.

Realisation in the "Aha!" Reflections is understanding that gratitude extends beyond external circumstances to internal growth and awareness.

6. The "Nature's Marvels" Photo Essay:
Grab your phone or camera for the "Nature's Marvels" Photo Essay. Take a stroll outdoors and capture the beauty around you – a blooming flower, a stunning sunset, or even a quirky squirrel doing acrobatics. Compile these photos in your journal, creating a visual feast of gratitude.
Nature offers a constant wellspring of beauty to be grateful for.

7. The "Comedy of Errors" Gratitude:
Indulge in the "Comedy of Errors" Gratitude. Recall a time when everything went hilariously wrong, and find reasons to be grateful for the comedy woven into the chaos. Laughter, after all, is the best seasoning for life's unpredictable moments.
Imperfection is a canvas for gratitude and amusement.

Journal Prompts:

1. Reflect on your Daily Delight List entries. How did acknowledging small joys impact your overall mood and perception of daily life?

2. Share your Marvellous Mishaps Chronicle. What mishap did you turn into a marvel, and how did it shift your perspective?

3. Write about your "Unexpected Kindness" Scavenger Hunt experiences. How did noticing and acknowledging acts of kindness enhance your connection to the world around you?

4. Explore your Past-Present-Future Love Letter. What past, present, and future moments did you express gratitude for, and how did it create a sense of continuity in your life?

5. Reflect on your "Aha!" Reflections. What realisations or insights have you recently gained, and how did expressing gratitude for them deepen your understanding of yourself?

6. Share your "Nature's Marvels" Photo Essay. What natural wonders did you capture, and how did the act of visually documenting them enhance your gratitude practice?

7. Write about your "Comedy of Errors" Gratitude experience. How did finding humour in a chaotic situation contribute to your ability to accept imperfections with grace?

Remember, my glittery gratitude enthusiasts, journaling isn't about creating a flawless masterpiece. It's about embracing the messiness of life with gratitude as your guide.

Healing Through Creativity: Expressing Yourself Unapologetically

Creativity – the magical elixir that infuses life with colour, zest, and a healthy dose of quirkiness. As I've journeyed through the realms of exhaustion and self-discovery, I've come to realise that creativity isn't just about painting masterpieces or penning award-winning novels. No, it's about embracing your inner weirdo and letting your imagination run wild, unencumbered by the shackles of judgment or expectation.

So, my fellow weary warriors, let's plunge enthusiastically into the wonderfully wacky world of creative expression and discover how it can serve as a powerful tool on our path to acceptance and vitality.

1. Doodle Delirium:
Grab a blank sheet of paper and a handful of colourful markers, and let's indulge in a little doodle therapy. Set a timer for ten minutes and unleash your inner artiste. Don't overthink it – just let your pen dance across the page in whatever way feels right. Whether it's whimsical swirls, funky patterns, or abstract shapes, let your creativity flow freely. When the timer dings, take a step back and admire your masterpiece. Embrace the imperfections, celebrate the quirks, and revel in the joy of self-expression.

2. Dance Party Extravaganza:
Who says you need to be a trained dancer to bust a move? Crank up your favourite playlist, clear some space in your living room, and let's boogie! Throw caution to the wind and dance like

nobody's watching – because, let's face it, nobody is (unless you have nosy neighbours with binoculars, in which case, dance even harder). Lose yourself in the music, feel the rhythm pulsating through your veins, and embrace the sheer silliness of it all. Bonus points for incorporating spontaneous air guitar solos and interpretive dance moves.

3. Write Like Nobody's Reading:
Grab a journal or open a new document on your computer, and let's engage in a little writing therapy. Set a timer for fifteen minutes and let your thoughts spill onto the page without censorship or judgment. Write about your day, your dreams, your deepest fears – whatever comes to mind. Don't worry about grammar, punctuation, or coherence; this is your safe space to unleash your inner monologue in all its messy glory. When the timer goes off, take a moment to reread what you've written and marvel at the raw beauty of your unfiltered thoughts.

4. DIY Delights:
Channel your inner Martha Stewart and embark on a DIY adventure of epic proportions. Whether it's crafting homemade candles, sculpting mini clay figurines, or knitting cozy scarves, pick a project that speaks to your soul and dive in headfirst. Embrace the therapeutic rhythm of creation as you lose yourself in the tactile sensations of molding, shaping, and crafting. Revel in the satisfaction of bringing something beautiful into existence with your own two hands, and relish in the joy of creating something uniquely yours.

5. Embrace Your Inner Child:
Remember the carefree days of childhood when imagination reigned supreme and the world was your playground? Tap into that inner child and indulge in a little playful escapism. Build a fort

out of blankets and pillows, engage in a spirited game of tag with your inner circle, or lose yourself in a whimsical storybook adventure. Let go of inhibitions, embrace the absurd, and revel in the simple pleasures of silliness and spontaneity.

As we bask in the glow of our creative endeavours, let's take a moment to reflect on the transformative power of self-expression. Through creativity, we unlock hidden depths of authenticity, vulnerability, and resilience. We embrace our quirks, celebrate our uniqueness, and honour the beautifully messy tapestry of our inner worlds. So, my fellow weary warriors, let's continue to unleash our creativity with wild abandon and express ourselves unapologetically, for in doing so, we reclaim our vitality and embrace the full spectrum of our humanity.

Journal Prompts:

1. How did you feel while engaging in the creative exercises? Did any emotions or memories surface during the process?

2. Reflect on a time when you felt inhibited or judged in expressing your creativity. How did it impact you, and what insights did you gain from that experience?

3. Consider incorporating regular creative practices into your routine. What activities resonate with you, and how can you integrate them into your daily life?

4. Explore the concept of "creative acceptance" – embracing both the light and shadow aspects of your creativity. How can you cultivate a sense of acceptance and self-love in your creative pursuits?

5. Write a love letter to your inner artist, expressing gratitude for their boundless creativity, resilience, and unwavering courage.

Reimagining Productivity: Quality Over Quantity

We're about to embark on an epic expedition through the dense and daunting jungle of productivity. But fret not for amidst the tangled vines and treacherous terrain, I bring tidings of great joy: it's time to cast aside the dusty, dog-eared rulebook of productivity and adopt a revolutionary new paradigm. One that champions quality over quantity, sass over stress, and liberation over limitation.

Let's start by shining a spotlight on the insidious myth of productivity that has haunted us for far too long. Picture it: the relentless drumbeat of busyness, the glorification of multitasking, and the never-ending rat race to cram as many tasks as humanly possible into a single day. It's a narrative that's been drilled into our collective consciousness, whispering insidiously in our ears that our worth is tied to our productivity, and our value is measured by our ability to check off boxes on an endless to-do list.

But here's the truth, my friends: it's all a big, fat lie. We've been sold a bill of goods, hoodwinked by a societal construct that values quantity over quality and equates busyness with worthiness. And it's high time we called foul.

Acceptance plays a pivotal role in this revelation. We must first accept that we are not automatons programmed to churn out work endlessly. We are human beings, flawed and fallible, with finite reserves of time, energy, and attention. And you know what? That's perfectly okay. In fact, it's more than okay—it's beautiful. By embracing our humanity and acknowledging our limitations, we can liberate ourselves from the suffocating grip of the productivity myth and reclaim our sense of self-worth.

So let's raise our banners high and declare our independence from the tyranny of busyness. Let's cast off the shackles of expectation and forge a new path—one that honours the sanctity of our time and the sovereignty of our souls.

But wait, you might be thinking, does this mean we should abandon productivity altogether? Absolutely not. Productivity, when wielded wisely, can be a powerful tool for achieving our goals and manifesting our dreams. The key lies not in the quantity of our output, but in the quality of our efforts. It's about working smarter, not harder. It's about prioritising tasks that align with our values and goals, and letting go of those that don't serve us. It's about embracing the art of saying no, setting boundaries, and fiercely protecting our time and energy.

So let's embark on this journey together with our heads held high and our hearts ablaze with passion. Let's rewrite the narrative of productivity and reclaim our power to define success on our own terms. And above all, let's remember to approach this adventure with a healthy dose of humour, because after all, laughter is the best antidote to the pressures of modern life.

1. The Power of Prioritisation:
Grab a pen and a piece of paper (or your trusty digital planner, if you're more of a tech-savvy warrior), and let's dive into the exhilarating world of prioritisation. Take a moment to list out all the tasks swirling around in your mind like a frenzied tornado. Now, here's the fun part: circle the top three tasks that are absolutely essential for you to tackle today. These are your priorities—the golden nuggets amidst the chaos. Focus your energy and attention on these top three tasks, and watch as your productivity skyrockets without the overwhelm.

2. The Art of Saying No:
Repeat after me: "No" is not a dirty word. In fact, it's a powerful weapon in your arsenal against the tyranny of overcommitment. So, let's practice flexing our "no" muscles with confidence and grace. The next time someone asks you to take on an extra project, attend yet another Zoom meeting, or join a committee that you have zero interest in, channel your inner superhero and politely decline. Remember, every "no" is a "yes" to your own well-being and sanity.

3. The Joy of Single-Tasking:
In a world obsessed with multitasking, single-tasking is the rebellious act of rebellion we've all been craving. So, put down your phone, close all those unnecessary browser tabs, and let's

dive into the blissful simplicity of single-tasking. Choose one task to focus on and give it your undivided attention. Whether it's writing a report, folding laundry, or savouring a cup of coffee, immerse yourself fully in the present moment and revel in the joy of doing one thing at a time.

4. Embrace the Power of Imperfection:
Newsflash: perfectionism is overrated. Instead of striving for flawlessness, let's embrace the beautiful messiness of imperfection. Give yourself permission to make mistakes, take detours, and zigzag your way towards success. Remember, it's not about getting it right the first time—it's about learning, growing, and embracing the journey along the way.

5. Celebrate Your Wins, Big and Small:
In the relentless pursuit of productivity, it's easy to overlook our victories, no matter how small they may seem. So, let's take a moment to pause, reflect, and celebrate our wins, big and small. Whether it's finally finishing that project you've been procrastinating on, hitting your daily step goal, or simply getting out of bed and facing the day with courage, every achievement deserves to be acknowledged and celebrated.

Journal Prompts:

1. Reflect on your current approach to productivity. Are you prioritising quality over quantity, or are you stuck in the endless cycle of busyness? What insights can you glean from this reflection?

2. Consider the top three tasks on your to-do list. Are they truly essential, or are you filling your plate with unnecessary busywork? How can you prioritise your tasks more effectively to focus on what truly matters?

3. Explore your relationship with saying no. Are you comfortable setting boundaries and declining commitments that don't align with your priorities? How can you practice saying no with confidence and grace?

4. Reflect on a time when you embraced imperfection and allowed yourself to let go of the pressure to be perfect. What did you learn from that experience, and how can you incorporate more imperfection into your life?

5. Take a moment to celebrate your wins, big and small. What achievements are you proud of, and how can you honour and celebrate them?

The Role of Laughter: Finding Joy Amidst Life's Challenges

Welcome, my fellow adventurers, to an exhilarating exploration into the captivating world of laughter. Amidst life's turbulent storms, we stand armed with nothing but our trusty umbrella of humour, ready to navigate the tempestuous seas of existence with grace, resilience, and an abundance of laughter.

Let's embark on our journey with a robust belly laugh, shall we? Laughter isn't merely a fleeting amusement; it's a potent elixir with profound healing properties. Scientific research has shown that laughter triggers the release of endorphins, our body's natural feel-good chemicals, which can reduce pain, alleviate stress, and boost our overall sense of well-being. Furthermore, laughter stimulates the production of dopamine, a neurotransmitter associated with pleasure and reward, leading to a cascade of positive physiological and psychological effects.

Acceptance plays a crucial role in understanding the profound healing power of laughter. By embracing life's challenges with humour and resilience, we open ourselves up to the therapeutic benefits of laughter. Instead of resisting or resenting the obstacles in our path, we can choose to approach them with grace and acceptance, allowing laughter to serve as a beacon of light amidst the darkness.

Scientific evidence also suggests that laughter strengthens social bonds and fosters a sense of connection and belonging. Shared laughter promotes empathy, cooperation, and trust, enhancing our relationships with others and creating a supportive network of allies to weather life's storms together. In this way, laughter becomes a powerful tool for building resilience and cultivating acceptance in the face of adversity.

As we journey through life's ups and downs, let laughter be our steadfast companion, guiding us through the darkest of nights and illuminating the path to joy and fulfilment. Through acceptance, we can harness the transformative power of laughter to find solace, strength, and connection amidst life's challenges.

1. The Comedy Corner:

First up, we're heading to the comedy corner for a dose of humour therapy. Whether it's a stand-up special, a hilarious sitcom, or a collection of dad jokes, find something that tickles your funny bone and dive in headfirst. Allow yourself to be swept away by the infectious laughter of others and revel in the joy of shared hilarity. Bonus points for snorting, cackling, and doing that weird thing where you laugh so hard you cry.

2. The Laughter Journal

Next, it's time to bust out your trusty laughter journal and start documenting those moments of merriment. Whether it's a ridiculous pun, a spontaneous dance party in your living room, or a comically awkward encounter at the grocery store, jot down those moments that bring a smile to your face and a twinkle to your eye. Not only will this journal serve as a delightful pick-me-up on rainy days, but it will also serve as a reminder that laughter is never far away if you know where to look.

3. The Silly Selfie Challenge:

Now, here's a fun one: the silly selfie challenge. Grab your phone, strike your goofiest pose, and snap a selfie that would make even the most stoic statue crack a smile. Whether you're sporting a pair of oversized sunglasses, rocking a ridiculous hat, or making faces that would make your grandmother blush, embrace the absurdity and let your inner goofball shine. Bonus points for sharing your silliest selfies with friends and family to spread the joy far and wide.

4. The Laughter Meditation:

Close your eyes, take a deep breath, and prepare to embark on a journey into the heart of hilarity with the laughter meditation. Find a comfortable spot to sit or lie down, and allow yourself to sink into a state of relaxation. Now, imagine a tiny tickle monster perched on your shoulder, armed with an arsenal of feather dusters and whoopee cushions. With each inhale, feel the tickle monster's mischievous energy coursing through your body, filling you with warmth and joy. And with each exhale, release a burst of laughter that echoes through the cosmos. Allow the laughter to bubble up from deep within your belly and spill out into the universe, transforming your worries into giggles and your fears into chuckles.

5. The Gratitude Giggle Fest:
Last but not least, let's wrap things up with a gratitude giggle fest. Take a moment to reflect on all the things in your life that bring you joy, from the mundane to the miraculous. Whether it's the smell of freshly baked cookies, the warmth of a cozy blanket, or the sound of rain tapping against your window, allow yourself to bask in the glow of gratitude. And as you count your blessings, let each one be accompanied by a hearty chuckle of appreciation for the absurd beauty of life.

Journal Prompts:

1. Reflect on a time when laughter helped you navigate a difficult situation or find perspective amidst adversity. What insights did you gain from that experience, and how did it impact your outlook on life?

2. Consider incorporating more laughter into your daily routine. What activities bring you joy and make you laugh uncontrollably? How can you prioritise these moments of mirth in your life?

3. Explore the concept of acceptance through humour. How can laughter help you accept life's imperfections and find beauty in the absurdity of existence?

4. Reflect on the role of humour in your relationships. How does laughter strengthen your connections with others and deepen your sense of camaraderie? How can you cultivate a more lighthearted and playful attitude in your interactions with loved ones?

5. Take a moment to express gratitude for the gift of laughter. What are you thankful for, and how does laughter enrich your life on a daily basis?

As we navigate the unpredictable waters of existence, let's remember that laughter isn't just a luxury—it's a lifeline. So, my fellow adventurers, let's embrace the absurdity, find joy in the mundane, and laugh in the face of adversity. For in laughter, we find solace, strength, and the courage to face life's challenges with a smile on our faces and a twinkle in our eyes.

Mindful Eating: Savouring the Pleasures of Nourishment

Alright, fellow food enthusiasts, fasten your seatbelts and prepare your taste buds, because we're embarking on an indulgent odyssey into the world of mindful eating. We're surrounded by a symphony of tantalising aromas, an explosion of mouthwatering flavours, and an endless banquet of culinary delights stretching as far as the eye can see. But in the hustle and bustle of our hectic lives, how often do we truly pause to savour the simple pleasure of nourishment? Fear not, my friends, for I am here to serve as your culinary guide on a quest to rediscover the art of mindful eating—infused with acceptance, awareness, and a generous sprinkling of humour.

Let's begin by unraveling the mystery of mindful eating. Now, you might be thinking, "Mindful eating? Isn't that just a fancy term for paying attention to what you eat?" Well, yes and no. While mindful eating does involve being present and attentive during meals, it encompasses far more than simply chewing your food slowly. It's about cultivating a profound awareness of our relationship with food, embracing the sensory experience of eating, and fostering a deep sense of gratitude for the nourishment it provides.

Acceptance lies at the heart of mindful eating. In a world inundated with conflicting dietary advice, from the latest fad diets to the cult of superfoods promoted by social media influencers, it's crucial to recognise that there's no one-size-fits-all approach to nourishment. Mindful eating transcends the constraints of rigid rules and restrictive labels. Instead, it invites us to tune into our body's innate wisdom, integrity our individual cravings, and approach food with an attitude of curiosity, kindness, and compassion. It's about cultivating a harmonious relationship with food—one that celebrates diversity, indulges in pleasure, and honours the unique needs of our bodies and minds.

1. The Sensory Feast:
Our first step on this mindful eating adventure is the sensory feast. Set aside some time to prepare a simple meal or snack, focusing on fresh, whole ingredients that tantalise the senses. As you gather your ingredients and prepare your meal, pay attention to the colours, textures, and aromas that fill the air. Take a moment to appreciate the beauty of nature's bounty and the nourishment it provides for both body and soul.

Once your meal is ready, sit down at the table and take a few deep breaths to centre yourself. As you begin to eat, engage all of your senses in the experience. Notice the crunch of fresh vegetables, the warmth of a steaming bowl of soup, or the rich aroma of freshly brewed coffee. Savour each bite, allowing yourself to fully immerse in the sensory pleasures of nourishment.

2. The Mindful Bite:
Next up, we have the mindful bite. This exercise is all about slowing down and savouring each mouthful with intention and awareness. Before taking a bite, pause for a moment to observe your food. Notice its colours, textures, and aromas, and appreciate the effort that went into preparing it. Then, take a small bite and chew slowly, paying attention to the flavours and sensations that unfold in your mouth.

As you chew, try to resist the urge to rush through your meal. Instead, focus on the act of eating itself, relishing each bite as if it were the first. Notice how your body responds to the food—how it feels in your mouth, how it nourishes you, and how it makes you feel physically and emotionally. By practicing mindful eating in this way, you can cultivate a deeper appreciation for the food you consume and develop a healthier relationship with eating.

3. The Gratitude Plate:
Now, let's turn our attention to the gratitude plate. Before you begin your meal, take a moment to express gratitude for the food in front of you. Reflect on the journey it took to arrive on your plate—the farmers who grew it, the workers who harvested it, and the hands that prepared it. Acknowledge the nourishment it provides for your body and the pleasure it brings to your senses.

As you eat, continue to cultivate a sense of gratitude for each bite. With each mouthful, silently thank the food for the sustenance it provides and the joy it brings to your life. By infusing your meals with gratitude, you can deepen your connection to the food you eat and foster a greater appreciation for the abundance that surrounds you.

4. The Mindful Moment:
Finally, let's wrap things up with the mindful moment. Throughout the day, take time to check in with yourself and assess your hunger and fullness levels. Before reaching for a snack or sitting down to a meal, ask yourself: Am I truly hungry, or am I eating out of habit, boredom, or emotion? Tune into your body's signals and honour its cues, eating mindfully and with intention.

As you go about your day, practice bringing mindfulness to your eating habits. Notice the sensations of hunger and fullness, the taste and texture of the food you consume, and the emotions that arise before, during, and after meals. By cultivating awareness and acceptance in your eating habits, you can nourish your body, mind, and spirit in a way that promotes balance, vitality, and joy.

Journal Prompts:

1. Reflect on your current eating habits and consider how mindfulness could enhance your relationship with food. What are some challenges you face when it comes to eating mindfully, and how can you overcome them?

2. Explore the concept of acceptance in relation to food and eating. How can you practice accepting your body, your cravings, and your food choices without judgment or criticism?

3. Consider the role of gratitude in your eating habits. How does expressing gratitude for your food impact your overall experience of eating, and how can you incorporate more gratitude into your meals?

4. Reflect on any insights or observations you've gained from practicing mindful eating. How has this experience influenced your relationship with food, your body, and your overall well-being?

5. Take a moment to set intentions for incorporating more mindfulness into your eating habits moving forward. What specific actions can you take to cultivate a greater sense of awareness, acceptance, and gratitude in your approach to food and eating?

As we conclude our exploration of mindful eating, remember that this journey is not about perfection, but rather about progress and self-discovery. Embrace each moment with openness and curiosity, allowing yourself to savour the joys of nourishment and cultivate a deeper connection with the food you consume.

So, my fellow food enthusiasts, let's raise our forks to the delicious adventure that lies ahead—bon appétit!

Accepting Change: The Constant in Life's Equation

Imagine life as a vast, swirling ocean, with waves of transformation crashing upon the shores of our existence. From the exhilarating highs of new beginnings to the daunting lows of unexpected endings, change is the one constant in the ever-shifting landscape of our lives.

Let's embark on this journey by confronting the unwavering truth: change is as inevitable as the rising sun and the changing of the seasons. No matter how fiercely we cling to the familiar comforts of the present, life has a funny way of nudging us out of our comfort zones and into the unknown. Whether it's a new job opportunity that propels us into uncharted territory, the heartache of a breakup that leaves us feeling adrift, or the global upheaval of a pandemic that reshapes our world in profound ways, change is the force that propels us forward on the journey of self-discovery and growth.

Acceptance is our ally in navigating the turbulent waters of change. Instead of resisting the currents of transformation like a stubborn boulder in a rushing river, we must learn to surrender to the ebb and flow of life's ever-changing tide. For change is not our enemy; it is our greatest teacher, offering lessons in resilience, adaptability, and the art of letting go. By embracing change with open arms and a spirit of curiosity, we unlock its transformative power and discover the boundless opportunities it brings for personal evolution and renewal.

In the face of life's unpredictable twists and turns, acceptance becomes our compass, guiding us through the maze of uncertainty with grace and resilience. As we navigate the peaks and valleys of our journey, let us remember that change is not a threat to be feared, but a gift to be embraced—a testament to the resilience of the human spirit and the limitless potential for growth and transformation that resides within each of us.

So, let us embark on this journey with courage, curiosity, and an unwavering belief in our ability to weather life's storms and emerge stronger, wiser, and more resilient than ever before. For in the embrace of change lies the promise of new beginnings, unforeseen opportunities, and the boundless potential of the human spirit.

1. The Change Journal:

Our first order of business is to grab a notebook and start jotting down our thoughts, feelings, and observations about change. I call it the Change Journal—a sacred space where we can document our ever-evolving relationship with the inevitable twists and turns of life.

Here's how it works: Set aside a few minutes each day to reflect on the changes happening in your life, both big and small. How are you reacting to these changes? Are you embracing them with open arms, or are you resisting them like a cat being dragged into a bathtub? Write down your thoughts, feelings, and any insights you gain from these reflections. By cultivating awareness and acceptance through journaling, you can navigate the ups and downs of life with greater resilience and grace.

2. The Change Mindset:

Next up, let's shift our mindset from one of resistance to one of acceptance. Instead of viewing change as a threat to our stability and security, let's reframe it as an opportunity for growth and transformation. I like to call this the Change Mindset—a mental shift that empowers us to embrace change with confidence and curiosity.

To cultivate the Change Mindset, start by challenging your beliefs about change. Ask yourself: What stories am I telling myself about change? Are these stories serving me, or are they holding me back? By examining the narratives we've constructed around change, we can identify any limiting beliefs and replace them with empowering ones that foster acceptance and resilience.

3. The Change Compass:
Now, let's equip ourselves with a powerful tool for navigating the tumultuous seas of change: the Change Compass. Think of the Change Compass as your trusty navigational guide, helping you chart a course through life's ever-shifting landscape with clarity and purpose.

To create your Change Compass, start by identifying your values and priorities in life. What matters most to you? What are your non-negotiables? Once you've clarified your values, use them as your North Star to guide your decisions and actions in the face of change. Ask yourself: Does this change align with my values and priorities? If not, how can I adapt and respond in a way that honours who I am and what I stand for?

4. The Change Celebration:
Finally, let's celebrate change like it's New Year's Eve and we just won the lottery. That's right, my friends—it's time to throw a Change Celebration, complete with confetti, champagne, and maybe a little interpretive dance.

Gather your friends, family, or even just your pet goldfish, and toast to the inevitability of change. Share stories of the changes you've experienced and how they've shaped you into the resilient, badass warrior you are today. By celebrating change with laughter and love, we not only honour the past but also embrace the limitless possibilities of the future.

Journal Prompts:

1. Reflect on a recent change in your life and explore your initial reactions to it. How did you respond to the change?

Were you able to accept it with grace, or did you struggle with resistance?

2. Consider the stories you tell yourself about change and how they influence your mindset. Are these stories empowering or limiting? How can you rewrite these narratives to foster greater acceptance and resilience?
3. Identify one value or priority that guides your decisions and actions in the face of change. How does this value support you in navigating life's uncertainties with courage and grace?

4. Imagine yourself embracing change with open arms, curiosity, and excitement. What opportunities for growth and transformation might emerge from this mindset shift?

5. Take a moment to express gratitude for the changes you've experienced and the lessons they've taught you. How have these changes shaped you into the resilient, adaptable person you are today?

As we wrap up our exploration of accepting change, remember that life is a wild and unpredictable adventure, full of twists, turns, and unexpected detours. By embracing change with open arms, cultivating a mindset of acceptance, and navigating with grace and humour, we can ride the waves of uncertainty with confidence and resilience.

Nature as a Therapist: Connecting with the Vitality of the Outdoors

It's time to lace up our hiking boots, slather on some sunscreen, and venture into the great outdoors. Picture this: we're surrounded by towering trees, serenaded by the melodious chirping of birds, and basking in the warm embrace of sunshine. But amidst the hustle and bustle of modern life, how often do we truly connect with the healing power of nature? I'm here to guide you on a journey to rediscover the vitality and serenity that Mother Nature has to offer—all while embracing acceptance, of course.

Let's kick things off by diving headfirst into the therapeutic wonderland that is the great outdoors. Nature isn't just a pretty backdrop for our Instagram selfies—it's a powerful healer that offers solace for the weary soul, a balm for the stressed-out mind, and a sanctuary for the overworked body. From the restorative embrace of a forest bath to the invigorating rush of a mountain hike, nature has a magical way of rejuvenating our spirits and reconnecting us with the essence of our being.

In a world obsessed with productivity and constant stimulation, it's easy to overlook the simple pleasures of nature and dismiss them as frivolous indulgences. But by accepting nature as a vital component of our overall well-being, we open ourselves up to a world of healing possibilities. So let's swap our screens for sunsets, our deadlines for daisies, and our stress for starlit skies as we embark on a journey to embrace the therapeutic wonders of the great outdoors.

1. The Nature Walk:
Our first step on this journey to nature's embrace is the humble Nature Walk—a simple yet powerful practice that invites us to slow down, tune in, and reconnect with the natural world around us.

Find a nearby park, nature reserve, or even just a tree-lined street, and set aside some time for a leisurely stroll. As you walk, pay attention to your surroundings—the rustle of leaves in the breeze, the scent of wildflowers in the air, the vibrant colours of the landscape. Allow yourself to be fully present in the moment, savouring the sights, sounds, and sensations of nature with mindfulness and acceptance.

2. The Nature Meditation:
Next up, let's deepen our connection with nature through the practice of Nature Meditation—a gentle yet profound technique that allows us to quiet the mind, open the heart, and attune to the rhythms of the natural world.

Find a quiet spot in nature—a secluded meadow, a tranquil beach, or even just a shady corner of your backyard—and settle into a comfortable position. Close your eyes and take a few deep breaths, allowing yourself to relax and unwind. As you breathe, imagine yourself surrounded by the beauty and tranquility of nature, feeling the earth beneath you, the sun on your skin, and the gentle caress of the breeze.

3. The Nature Immersion:
Now, let's take our nature practice to the next level with the Nature Immersion—a full sensory experience that engages all five senses and invites us to fully immerse ourselves in the natural world.

Find a quiet spot in nature where you can sit or lie down comfortably—a grassy meadow, a shady grove of trees, or a peaceful lakeside. Close your eyes and take a moment to centre yourself, then begin to explore your surroundings with each of your senses. Notice the texture of the ground beneath you, the scent of the air, the sound of birdsong in the distance, the taste of the breeze on your lips, and the play of light and shadow through your closed eyelids. Allow yourself to be fully present in the moment, surrendering to the beauty and wonder of the natural world with acceptance and gratitude.

4. The Nature Connection:
Finally, let's cultivate a deeper connection with nature by incorporating it into our daily lives in meaningful and practical ways.

Start by spending time outdoors each day, whether it's a morning walk in the park, an al fresco lunch break, or an evening stroll under the stars. Look for opportunities to engage with nature in your everyday activities—planting a garden, birdwatching from your balcony, or simply taking a moment to pause and appreciate the beauty of a blooming flower.

Journal Prompts:

1. Reflect on your relationship with nature and how it impacts your overall well-being. How do you feel when you spend time outdoors? What benefits do you notice from connecting with nature?

2. Consider any barriers or challenges you face in incorporating nature into your daily life. What steps can you take to overcome these obstacles and prioritise spending time in nature?

3. Explore the concept of acceptance in relation to nature. How can you practice accepting and appreciating the beauty of the natural world, even in moments of discomfort or inconvenience?

4. Reflect on any insights or observations you've gained from practicing the exercises in this chapter. How has connecting with nature enriched your life and contributed to your sense of vitality and well-being?

5. Take a moment to express gratitude for the healing power of nature and the abundance of beauty and wonder it offers. What are you grateful for in your connection with the natural world, and how can you continue to nurture and cultivate this relationship in the future?

As we come to the end of our exploration into the therapeutic wonders of nature, let's carry forward the wisdom gained and the joys experienced. Remember, nature isn't just a destination—it's an ongoing journey, a constant wellspring of healing and rejuvenation. By embracing the outdoors with acceptance and gratitude, we deepen our connection to the natural world and enhance our lives in profound ways. So, my fellow adventurers, let's continue to seek solace and inspiration in the beauty of nature, allowing its boundless splendour to nourish our souls and invigorate our spirits. Until our next adventure, may you find peace, joy, and vitality in the embrace of the great outdoors.

Visualisation Techniques: Envisioning a Vibrant Future

Armed with nothing but our imagination and an unyielding resolve to bring our wildest dreams to life, we're about to embark on an extraordinary journey. But in a world inundated with endless to-do lists and pressing deadlines, how often do we pause to imagine the vibrant future we truly desire? Do not be afraid, my friends, for I am present to lead you on a mesmerising odyssey through the power of visualisation, while also embracing acceptance with open arms.

Let's begin by unraveling the mysteries surrounding visualisation. While some may dismiss it as mere daydreaming, scientific research has illuminated the profound effects of visualisation on our brains and behaviour. Neuroscientific studies have shown that when we vividly imagine ourselves accomplishing our goals or living our desired reality, our brain interprets these mental images as real experiences, activating the same neural pathways as if we were physically performing the actions. This phenomenon, known as "mental rehearsal," can significantly enhance our performance, boost our confidence, and improve our overall well-being.

Furthermore, research in the field of positive psychology has highlighted the transformative power of visualisation in shaping our mindset and outcomes. By visualising positive outcomes and cultivating a sense of optimism and possibility, we can rewire our brains to focus on opportunities and solutions, rather than dwelling on obstacles or setbacks. Studies have demonstrated that individuals who regularly practice visualisation experience greater resilience, lower levels of stress, and increased levels of motivation and perseverance.

Moreover, visualisation has been shown to have tangible effects on various aspects of our lives, from academic achievement to sports performance and even health outcomes. Athletes who incorporate visualisation into their training routines have been found to improve their skills, enhance their focus, and recover from injuries more rapidly. Similarly, students who visualise themselves succeeding academically are more likely to achieve higher grades and academic goals.

In a world driven by instant gratification and relentless pursuit of success, it's easy to dismiss visualisation as mere wishful thinking or new-age mysticism. However, by embracing the science-backed benefits of visualisation as a legitimate tool for personal growth and transformation, we can open ourselves up to a world of infinite possibilities.

Acceptance involves acknowledging and embracing our present circumstances, while also envisioning a brighter future. It's about trusting in the process of visualisation, even in the face of doubt or uncertainty, and surrendering to the belief that our dreams are within reach. By cultivating acceptance, we create space for creativity, inspiration, and manifestation to flow effortlessly into our lives.

So, my fellow dreamers, let us embark on this exhilarating journey with open hearts and minds, knowing that the visions we hold in our minds have the power to shape our reality. As we delve deeper into the enchanting world of visualisation, may we embrace acceptance as our guiding principle, allowing our dreams to unfold with grace and ease. After all, the magic of visualisation lies not only in its ability to transform our reality but also in our willingness to accept and embrace the wondrous possibilities that await us.

1. The Dream Board:
Our first step on this whimsical journey is the creation of a Dream Board—a visual masterpiece that serves as a tangible representation of our dreams, goals, and aspirations.

Grab a cork-board, poster board, or even just a blank wall space, and gather magazines, newspapers, photographs, and any other materials that inspire you. Start by envisioning your ideal future— what do you want to achieve, experience, or manifest in your life? Then, cut out images, words, and phrases that resonate with your vision and arrange them on your board in a way that feels intuitive and meaningful.

2. The Future Self Visualisation:
Next up, let's embark on a journey to meet our Future Self—a powerful visualisation exercise that allows us to step into the shoes of our future selves and experience the vibrant reality we desire.

Find a quiet space where you can relax and unwind, then close your eyes and take a few deep breaths to centre yourself. Imagine yourself five, ten, or even twenty years into the future, living your ideal life. What does it look like? Where are you? Who are you with? What are you doing?

3. The Scripting Technique:
Now, let's put pen to paper and bring our dreams to life with the Scripting Technique—a playful yet powerful exercise that involves

writing a detailed script of our desired reality as if it has already come to fruition.

Grab a journal, notebook, or even just a blank sheet of paper, and start writing about your dream life with vivid detail and unwavering belief. Describe your ideal day from start to finish— where you wake up, what you do, who you spend time with, and how you feel. Be as specific and detailed as possible, allowing yourself to immerse in the fantasy of your ideal reality with gusto and enthusiasm.

4. The Visualisation Meditation:
Finally, let's deepen our connection with our dreams through the practice of Visualisation Meditation—a gentle yet profound technique that allows us to quiet the mind, open the heart, and align with the energy of our desires.

Find a comfortable position, close your eyes, and take a few deep breaths to relax and centre yourself. Then, begin to visualise your desired reality with clarity and focus, allowing yourself to fully immerse in the sights, sounds, and sensations of your dream life. Engage all your senses as you immerse yourself in this vision, allowing yourself to fully experience the sights, sounds, smells, tastes, and sensations. As you meditate, cultivate a sense of gratitude and acceptance for the abundance that is already on its way to you, trusting in the power of visualisation to manifest your deepest desires.

Journal Prompts:

1. Reflect on your experience with visualisation techniques and how they have impacted your life. Have you noticed any shifts or changes in your mindset, behaviour, or circumstances as a result of practicing visualisation?

2. Consider any limiting beliefs or doubts that may be holding you back from fully embracing the power of visualisation. How can you cultivate acceptance and trust in the process, even in the face of uncertainty or skepticism?

3. Explore your dreams and aspirations for the future, and consider how visualisation can help you bring them to life. What do you want to achieve, experience, or manifest in your life, and how can visualisation support you on this journey?

4. Take a moment to visualise your ideal future with clarity and intention. What does it look like? How does it feel? What steps can you take to align with this vision and bring it into reality?

As we conclude our whimsical journey through the magical world of visualisation, let us carry forward the spark of imagination and the power of intention. Remember, the visions we hold in our minds have the potential to shape our reality and manifest our dreams into existence. By embracing acceptance and trust in the process of visualisation, we unleash our creative potential and invite abundance, joy, and fulfilment into our lives. So, my fellow dreamers, keep dreaming big, keep visualising boldly, and watch as the vibrant future you envision unfolds before your very eyes.

Decluttering for Clarity: Simplifying Life for Inner Peace

We're about to embark on an enlightening odyssey through the chaotic labyrinth of decluttering. Our lives resemble a hoarder's paradise, with piles of possessions threatening to topple over at every turn. I'm leading you to a tranquil haven of inner peace—all while embracing the liberating power of acceptance.

Let's shine a light on the comical chaos that clutter inflicts upon our lives. Who among us hasn't spent countless hours digging through overstuffed closets, only to emerge empty-handed and more frazzled than before? Or found ourselves buried beneath a mountain of paperwork, struggling to distinguish between essential documents and long-forgotten receipts? Clutter has a knack for sneaking up on us when we least expect it, transforming our once tidy homes into battlegrounds of disorder and disarray.

Acceptance is the cornerstone of our journey. It's time to acknowledge that clutter is an inevitable aspect of modern life. Whether it's a mishmash of mismatched socks or a towering stack of unopened mail, clutter is an ever-present companion on our journey through existence. However, instead of waging an endless war against it like a contestant on a reality TV show, why not greet it with open arms? By embracing the chaos for what it is —a fleeting inconvenience rather than a permanent state of being—we can reclaim our sanity and restore order to our lives.

So, my fellow clutter aficionados, let us embark on this expedition with courage and humour, knowing that by embracing acceptance, we can navigate the maze of clutter with grace and dignity. Together, we'll emerge victorious, with clutter banished and inner peace restored.

1. The Great Closet Clean-Out:
Our first step on this decluttering adventure is the Great Closet Clean-Out—a daring mission to conquer the chaos lurking within our wardrobes.

Grab a trash bag, put on your favourite playlist, and dive headfirst into the depths of your closet. Start by ruthlessly decluttering items that no longer serve you, whether it's clothes that haven't seen the light of day in years or accessories that have lost their luster. As you sift through the clutter, ask yourself: Does this spark joy? If the answer is no, bid it farewell and toss it into the "donate" pile with a flourish.

2. The Paper Purge:
Next up, let's tackle the Paper Purge—a Herculean task that involves vanquishing the stacks of paperwork threatening to engulf our desks and countertops.

Arm yourself with a shredder, recycling bin, and a healthy dose of determination, then dive into the paperwork abyss. Sort through each document with ruthless efficiency, separating the wheat from the chaff with precision. Remember: most of those receipts and old bills can be safely consigned to the recycling bin, while important documents can be filed away in a sleek and organised manner. As you declutter, revel in the satisfaction of restoring order to your paper kingdom.

3. The Kitchen Cleanup:

Let's shake things up with a Kitchen Cleanup—a culinary crusade to declutter our cooking spaces and reclaim our sanity amidst the chaos of pots, pans, and pantry staples.

Don your favourite apron, grab a sponge and a trash bag, and get ready to tackle the heart of your home—the kitchen. Start by emptying out your cabinets and drawers, one at a time, and sorting through the culinary chaos. Bid farewell to expired spices, chipped dishes, and gadgets you haven't touched since the Stone Age. As you declutter, channel your inner master chef and visualise the streamlined, efficient kitchen of your dreams.

Journal Prompts:

1. Reflect on your experience with decluttering and how it has impacted your sense of inner peace and well-being. What insights have you gained about your relationship with material possessions, and how can you cultivate a greater sense of acceptance and gratitude for the things that truly matter?

2. Consider any resistance or challenges you encountered during the decluttering process. How can you apply the principles of acceptance and mindfulness to overcome these obstacles and create a clutter-free environment that nurtures your soul?

3. Explore your vision for a clutter-free kitchen that nourishes both body and soul. What cooking habits or rituals can you incorporate into your daily routine to maintain a sense of order and serenity in your culinary domain?

As we journey through the whimsical world of decluttering, let's remember that the path to inner peace is paved with acceptance and humour. By embracing the chaos of clutter with open arms, we not only reclaim control over our physical spaces but also cultivate a sense of tranquility within ourselves. So, my cluttered comrades, let's bid farewell to the cluttered chaos of yesterday and welcome a brighter, more organised tomorrow with arms wide open.

Mindful Technology Use: Reclaiming Time for Meaningful Connection

Okay, fasten your seatbelts, fellow tech enthusiasts, as we're about to set off on a delightfully illuminating adventure through the digital wilderness of mindful tech utilisation. Our lives are a whirlwind of notifications, screens, and endless scrolling, leaving us feeling more disconnected than everHowever, don't worry, my companions, because I am here to navigate you through the maze of technology with cleverness, insight, and a generous amount of understanding.

Let's kick things off by shedding light on the comical chaos that technology brings into our lives. I mean, who hasn't accidentally sent a text to the wrong person or experienced the dreaded "butt dial" at the most inopportune moment? And let's not even get started on the endless stream of memes, cat videos, and viral TikToks that lure us into the digital abyss. Technology has a way of both enchanting and ensnaring us, leaving us simultaneously entertained and exasperated.

It's time to acknowledge that technology is an integral part of modern life, for better or for worse. Whether we're navigating the treacherous waters of social media or wrestling with the latest software update, technology is here to stay. But instead of succumbing to its seductive allure or railing against its pitfalls, why not approach it with a sense of humour and a spirit of acceptance? By embracing technology as a tool for connection and empowerment, rather than a source of stress or distraction, we can reclaim our time and prioritise meaningful connections in our digital age.

1. Digital Detox:
Our first step on this journey to mindful technology use is a Digital Detox—a daring adventure to disconnect from the digital world and reconnect with the present moment.

Set aside a designated period of time, whether it's a few hours, a day, or even a weekend, to unplug from your devices. Turn off your smartphone, silence your notifications, and resist the urge to check social media or email. Instead, engage in activities that nourish your mind, body, and soul, whether it's going for a nature walk, practicing mindfulness meditation, or enjoying quality time with loved ones. As you detox from the digital noise, notice how it feels to be fully present in the moment, free from the constant barrage of screens and distractions.

2. Tech-Free Zones:

Next up, let's create some Tech-Free Zones in our homes—a sanctuary where technology takes a backseat and human connection takes centre stage.

Designate specific areas in your home, such as the dining room table or the bedroom, as tech-free zones where screens are strictly prohibited. Use this space to engage in meaningful conversations, enjoy leisurely meals, or simply unwind without the intrusion of technology. Experiment with different activities, such as reading a book, playing board games, or practicing a hobby, to rediscover the joy of analog pursuits and deepen your connections with those around you. As you embrace these tech-free zones, savour the moments of genuine connection and intimacy that arise when technology is temporarily put on hold.

3. Mindful Screen Time:

Lastly, let's practice Mindful Screen Time—a conscious approach to using technology that prioritises intentionality and presence over mindless scrolling.

Before reaching for your device, pause for a moment and ask yourself: What am I hoping to gain from this screen time? Am I seeking information, entertainment, or connection? Set clear intentions for your tech usage and limit your time accordingly, being mindful of how each interaction contributes to your overall well-being. Practice self-awareness as you engage with technology, noticing any feelings of distraction, overwhelm, or FOMO that arise, and gently redirect your attention back to the present moment. By cultivating mindfulness in your screen time, you can harness the power of technology to enrich your life and deepen your connections with others.

Journal Prompts:

1. Reflect on your relationship with technology and how it impacts your daily life. What are some areas where you feel technology enhances your well-being, and where do you feel it detracts from your quality of life? How can you cultivate greater acceptance and mindfulness in your use of technology?

2. Consider your experiences with the Digital Detox, Tech-Free Zones, and Mindful Screen Time exercises. What insights did you gain about your relationship with technology, and how did these practices influence your sense of connection, presence, and well-being?

3. Explore your vision for a balanced and intentional approach to technology use. What habits or boundaries can you implement to ensure that technology enhances rather than detracts from your life? How can you prioritise meaningful connections and experiences in the digital age?

As we navigate the digital landscape with humour and acceptance, let's remember that technology is a powerful tool that can enrich our lives when used mindfully. By reclaiming our time and prioritising meaningful connections over mindless scrolling, we can cultivate deeper relationships, foster genuine moments of joy, and find greater fulfilment in our digital age. So, my tech-savvy comrades, let's embrace the whimsical adventure of mindful technology use with open hearts knowing that by doing so, we can reclaim our time for what truly matters—meaningful connections and moments of genuine presence.

The Power of Rituals: Grounding Yourself in Daily Practices

So, my dear tired-but-not-lazy comrades, let's talk about rituals. No, not the kind involving chanting under a full moon or sacrificing your favourite coffee mug to the caffeine gods. I'm talking about the everyday routines and practices that anchor us in the whirlwind of life, helping us stay grounded, centred, and maybe even a little less frazzled.

Now, I get it. When you're dragging yourself out of bed in the morning, the last thing you want to think about is establishing some elaborate morning routine that involves sunrise yoga and green smoothies. Trust me, I've been there. But hear me out – rituals don't have to be fancy or time-consuming. In fact, the simpler, the better.

Let's start with the morning, shall we? Instead of hitting the snooze button for the umpteenth time, try setting aside just five minutes for a mindful moment. Sit up, stretch, and take a few deep breaths. Maybe even give yourself a little pep talk in the mirror.

Next up, let's talk about meals. Now, I'm not saying you have to become a gourmet chef overnight (unless, of course, that's your thing), but taking the time to prepare and savour your food can do wonders for your energy levels and overall well-being. So, why not turn mealtime into a mini-celebration? Light a candle, put on some music, and actually taste your food instead of inhaling it while staring at your computer screen.

And let's not forget about bedtime. Instead of mindlessly scrolling through your phone until the wee hours of the morning (guilty as charged), try establishing a relaxing bedtime routine that signals to your body and mind that it's time to wind down. Maybe it's reading a few pages of a book, doing some gentle stretching, or simply jotting down a few things you're grateful for from the day.

Now, I know what you're thinking – all this talk of rituals sounds nice and all, but how is it supposed to help me reclaim my vitality? Well, my friend, here's the thing – rituals have a magical way of grounding us in the present moment, helping us cultivate a sense of mindfulness and intentionality in everything we do. And when we approach life from a place of presence and purpose, it becomes a whole lot easier to navigate the ups and downs with grace and resilience.

So, consider this your invitation to start incorporating some simple rituals into your daily routine. Experiment with different practices and see what resonates with you. And remember, it's not about adding more items to your to-do list or striving for perfection – it's about finding moments of joy, connection, and meaning in the midst of the chaos.

Now, I promised you some real practical exercises, didn't I? Here are a few ideas to get you started:

1. Morning Mindfulness:
Set aside five minutes each morning to sit quietly, focus on your breath, and set an intention for the day ahead. Bonus points if you can do it before checking your phone!

2. Mealtime Meditation:
Before diving into your next meal, take a moment to pause and express gratitude for the nourishment you're about to receive. Notice the colours, textures, and flavours of your food as you eat mindfully.

3. Bedtime Bliss:
Create a calming bedtime routine that signals to your body that it's time to wind down. This could include things like dimming the lights, taking a warm bath, or reading a few pages of a book.

4. Ritual Reflection:
At the end of each day, take a few minutes to reflect on your rituals and how they've impacted your energy levels and overall well-being. What worked well? What could use some tweaking? And most importantly, what moments of joy did you find along the way?

Journal Prompts:

1. What are some rituals or routines that currently exist in my daily life? How do they make me feel?

2. Are there any new rituals or practices I would like to incorporate into my routine? Why are they important to me?

3. How can I cultivate a sense of mindfulness and intentionality in my daily activities? What small changes can I make to bring more presence and purpose into my life?

4. Reflecting on my experiences with rituals, what have I learned about myself and my relationship with vitality? How can I continue to honour and nurture that relationship moving forward?

So there you have it – the power of rituals in reclaiming your vitality. So go forth and embrace the magic of everyday moments, one ritual at a time. You've got this!

Acceptance in Grief: Finding Peace in the Midst of Loss

Grief, a multifaceted emotional response to loss, represents a significant aspect of the human experience. While conventionally associated with bereavement, grief extends beyond the demise of a loved one, encompassing diverse forms of loss such as the dissolution of relationships, career setbacks, and unrealised aspirations. Despite its ubiquity, grief remains a complex and often bewildering phenomenon, characterised by a myriad of psychological, physiological, and behavioural manifestations.

Central to the process of navigating grief is the concept of acceptance. Unlike resignation or acquiescence, acceptance in the context of grief denotes the acknowledgment and integration of one's emotional reality, irrespective of its discomfort or intensity. This conceptual framework aligns with principles espoused in Acceptance and Commitment Therapy (ACT), a psychotherapeutic modality grounded in mindfulness and values clarification.

Research suggests that individuals who engage in acceptance-based approaches to grief experience lower levels of psychological distress and greater subjective well-being compared to those who adopt avoidant or suppressive coping strategies. By cultivating an attitude of acceptance towards their grief, individuals may attenuate maladaptive responses and facilitate adaptive adjustment processes.

In practical terms, acceptance involves the conscious recognition and validation of one's emotional experiences without judgment or resistance. This necessitates the cultivation of self-compassion and mindfulness, enabling individuals to observe their thoughts and feelings with equanimity and non-reactivity. Through the practice of acceptance, individuals can create psychological space for their grief, fostering an atmosphere of inner tranquility and emotional equanimity.

Now, here's the thing about grief – it's messy. Like, really messy. It's not a neat and tidy process with a clear beginning, middle, and end. Nope, grief is more like a rollercoaster ride through the seven circles of hell, complete with unexpected twists, turns, and stomach-churning drops. And just when you think you've reached the end of the ride, you realise you're right back where you started – feeling like you've been hit by a truckload of emotional baggage.

So, how do we make peace with this hot mess of emotions we call grief? Well, my friends, it all comes down to acceptance. Now, I know what you're thinking – "Acceptance? Seriously? You want me to just roll over and let grief steamroll me into oblivion?" Not exactly. Acceptance isn't about resigning yourself to a lifetime of misery and despair. It's about acknowledging the reality of your situation, embracing your feelings, and finding a way to move forward with grace and resilience.

Let me break it down for you with a little analogy. Think of grief as a stubborn houseguest who refuses to leave no matter how many times you drop hints about needing your space. You can try to ignore them, fight them, or drown them in cheap wine, but at the end of the day, they're still going to be there – lurking in the shadows, waiting for you to acknowledge their presence. And the sooner you do, the sooner you can start the process of healing.

So, how do we practice acceptance in the midst of grief? Well, my friends, I'm glad you asked. Here are a few real practical exercises to get you started:

1. Feel the Feels:
First things first – give yourself permission to feel whatever you're feeling. Whether it's sadness, anger, guilt, or all of the above, don't try to push your emotions away or pretend they don't exist. Instead, allow yourself to fully experience them, knowing that it's okay to not be okay.

2. Lean on Your Support System:
Grief can be a lonely journey, but you don't have to go it alone. Reach out to friends, family, or a therapist who can offer a listening ear, a shoulder to cry on, or a much-needed distraction from the pain.

3. Practice Self-Compassion:
Be gentle with yourself during this difficult time. Treat yourself with the same kindness and compassion you would offer to a dear friend who's going through a rough patch. And remember, it's okay to take things one day at a time – or even one breath at a time, if that's what it takes.

4. Find Meaning in the Mess:
While grief may feel like the end of the world, it can also be an opportunity for growth and transformation. Look for moments of beauty, grace, and wisdom amidst the chaos, and allow yourself to find meaning in the midst of the mess.

Journal Prompts:

1. What are some losses or transitions I've experienced recently that have triggered feelings of grief? How have these losses impacted me emotionally, physically, and spiritually?

2. How have I been coping with my grief so far? What strategies have been helpful, and which ones have been less effective?

3. What are some emotions or thoughts about my grief that I've been avoiding or suppressing? How can I begin to acknowledge and accept these feelings with compassion and curiosity?

4. Reflecting on my journey with grief, what are some lessons or insights I've gained about myself, my relationships, and the nature of loss? How can I use this newfound wisdom to navigate future challenges with grace and resilience?

So there you have it – a crash course in acceptance in the midst of loss. Remember, grief may be messy, painful, and downright ugly at times, but it's also a testament to the depth of our love and our capacity for resilience. So let's embrace it, ugly-cry and all, and trust that healing is possible, one step at a time.

The Liberation in Saying "Yes" to Self-Care

Let's talk about self-care. And no, I'm not just talking about slapping on a face mask and calling it a day (although, let's be real, that can be pretty darn satisfying). I'm talking about the kind of self-care that involves saying "yes" to yourself – even when everything and everyone else is screaming "no."

Now, I know what you're thinking – "But Emily, I'm too busy to take care of myself! I've got deadlines to meet, bills to pay, and a never-ending to-do list that's threatening to swallow me whole." Trust me, I hear you. As a recovering people-pleaser and chronic overachiever, I know what it's like to put everyone else's needs above your own, until you're running on fumes and praying for a miracle.

But here's the thing – self-care isn't selfish. In fact, it's one of the most radical acts of self-love you can engage in. Because when you prioritise your own well-being, you're not just doing yourself a favour – you're setting the stage for a happier, healthier, and more fulfilling life. And who wouldn't want a piece of that?

So, let's start by redefining what self-care actually looks like. Hint: it's not just about bubble baths and scented candles (although those can certainly be part of the equation). Self-care is about honouring your physical, emotional, and mental needs, and giving yourself permission to prioritise them – guilt-free.

I get it – carving out time for self-care can feel like an uphill battle, especially when you're juggling a million different responsibilities. But here's the secret: self-care doesn't have to be complicated or time-consuming. In fact, some of the most powerful acts of self-care are also the simplest.

So, without further ado, here are a few real practical exercises to help you say "yes" to self-care and reclaim your sanity:

1. The Power of "No":
Ah, the elusive art of saying "no." As a recovering people-pleaser, I know how hard it can be to turn down requests and set boundaries – but trust me, it's a game-changer. So the next time someone asks you to take on an extra project, attend yet another Zoom meeting, or babysit their pet iguana, give yourself permission to say "no" without guilt or explanation. Your time and energy are precious commodities – spend them wisely.

2. The Joy of Journalling:
Grab a pen and paper (or your favourite journaling app) and spend a few minutes jotting down your thoughts, feelings, and reflections. Whether you're venting about a frustrating day at work, expressing gratitude for the little things, or simply doodling your heart out, journaling is a powerful tool for self-expression and self-discovery.

3. Move Your Body:
No, you don't have to run a marathon or contort yourself into a pretzel (unless, of course, that's your thing). Just find a form of movement that brings you joy – whether it's dancing around your living room to your favourite playlist, taking a leisurely stroll through the park, or practicing some gentle yoga stretches. Moving your body is not only good for your physical health – it's also a great way to boost your mood and relieve stress.

4. Treat Yo' Self:
Set aside some time each week to indulge in a little self-care treat. Whether it's treating yourself to a decadent dessert, splurging on a new book or movie, or pampering yourself with a DIY spa day at home, giving yourself permission to indulge in a little luxury can do wonders for your well-being.

Journal Prompts:

1. Reflect on your current relationship with self-care. How often do you prioritise your own needs and well-being? What are some barriers or challenges that prevent you from engaging in self-care on a regular basis?

2. Consider the ways in which you typically cope with stress and overwhelm. Are these coping strategies sustainable and effective in promoting your overall well-being? What adjustments or alternatives could you explore to better support your self-care needs?

3. Explore any underlying beliefs or narratives that may be contributing to feelings of guilt or self-doubt around self-care. How can you challenge these beliefs and cultivate a more compassionate and accepting attitude towards prioritising your own needs?

4. Imagine your ideal self-care routine. What activities, practices, or rituals would you incorporate into your daily or weekly routine to nurture your physical, emotional, and mental well-being? How can you start taking steps towards implementing these practices in your life today?

In conclusion, saying "yes" to self-care is not just an act of kindness towards yourself – it's a revolutionary act of reclaiming your time, energy, and sanity in a world that often demands too much of us. So go ahead, embrace the liberation that comes with prioritising your own well-being, and remember: you deserve it. Say "yes" to self-care, and watch as your life transforms into a happier, healthier, and more fulfilling journey.

Building a Supportive Community: Connecting with Kindred Spirits

Community. No, I'm not talking about some hoity-toity exclusive club where you have to wear a fancy hat and recite the secret handshake. I'm talking about finding your tribe – those kindred spirits who lift you up, cheer you on, and make you snort-laugh milk out of your nose when you least expect it.

I'll be honest – building a supportive community isn't always a walk in the park. It's more like navigating a minefield of awkward small talk, social anxiety, and the occasional run-in with a well-meaning but slightly overbearing neighbour who insists on showing you their collection of commemorative spoons (true story, folks).

But here's the thing – when you find your tribe, it's like coming home to a warm hug and a bottomless plate of nachos.

Suddenly, you're not just surviving – you're thriving, buoyed by the love, laughter, and collective wisdom of your fellow misfits and weirdos.

So, how do we go about building this mythical tribe of ours? Well, my friends, it all starts with a little thing called vulnerability. Yep, you heard me right – vulnerability. As scary as it may seem, opening up and letting your guard down is the key to forging authentic connections with others.

I know what you're thinking – "I'd rather wrestle a pack of rabid squirrels than share my deepest fears and insecurities with another human being." As someone who's spent a good portion of her life hiding behind a carefully constructed facade of confidence and competence, vulnerability doesn't exactly come naturally to me either.

But vulnerability is not weakness. It's strength. It's courage. It's the willingness to show up, be seen, and be truly, unapologetically yourself – warts and all. And when you have the courage to be vulnerable, you create space for others to do the same, fostering an atmosphere of trust, authenticity, and mutual support.

So, here are a few exercises to help you build your own supportive community of kindred spirits:

1. Get Out of Your Comfort Zone:
Take a deep breath, summon your inner badass, and step outside your comfort zone. Whether it's joining a new club or organisation, attending a meet-up or networking event, or simply striking up a conversation with a stranger at the coffee shop,

challenge yourself to embrace discomfort and lean into the unknown.

2. Practice Active Listening:
Put down your phone, make eye contact, and actually listen to what the other person is saying (novel concept, I know). Practice active listening skills such as nodding, paraphrasing, and asking open-ended questions to show that you're engaged and interested in what they have to say.

3. Share Your Story:
Take a leap of faith and share your own story with others. Whether it's opening up about your struggles, triumphs, or embarrassing childhood mishaps, vulnerability begets vulnerability. By sharing your own experiences authentically, you invite others to do the same, fostering deeper connections and mutual understanding.

4. Cultivate Empathy:
Put yourself in the shoes of others and practice empathy and compassion. Recognise that everyone has their own struggles and challenges, and seek to understand their perspectives without judgment or criticism. Offer support, validation, and encouragement to those who need it most, and be willing to lend a helping hand or a listening ear whenever possible.

Journal Prompts:

1. Reflect on your current social support network. Who are the people in your life that you turn to for support, encouragement, and companionship? How do these relationships contribute to your overall well-being and sense of belonging?

2. Consider the qualities and characteristics you value most in a supportive community. What are some common values, interests, or experiences that you seek in potential kindred spirits? How can you actively seek out and cultivate connections with individuals who share these traits?

3. Explore any fears or insecurities that may be holding you back from building deeper connections with others. What limiting beliefs or negative self-talk patterns are undermining your confidence and self-worth? How can you challenge these beliefs and cultivate a greater sense of self-compassion and acceptance?

4. Imagine your ideal supportive community. What does it look like, sound like, and feel like? What activities, rituals, or shared experiences would characterise this community? How can you take concrete steps towards building and nurturing this community in your own life?

Building a supportive community isn't just about finding people who share your interests or hobbies – it's about finding kindred spirits who accept you for who you are, flaws and all. So embrace vulnerability, step out of your comfort zone, and open your heart to the possibility of authentic connections. Because when you find your tribe, you'll discover that you're not just surviving – you're thriving, buoyed by the love, laughter, and collective wisdom of those who truly understand and support you. Say "yes" to building your tribe, and watch as your life becomes infinitely richer and more fulfilling.

The Journey of Self-Discovery: Accepting and Embracing Change

We're strapping ourselves in for a thrilling ride through the tumultuous yet transformative landscape of self-discovery. Life's tossing us curveballs faster than a rookie pitcher in the World Series, and we're at bat, ready to knock those challenges right out of the park. But fret not, my friends, because I'm here to be your trusty guide as we navigate the twists and turns of self-discovery with humour, grace, and a hefty dose of acceptance.

Let's plunge into the whirlwind of change. It's that unavoidable force that swoops into our lives like a whirlwind, rearranging the furniture without so much as a warning. Whether it's a new job opportunity, a relationship ending, or unexpected turns in our plans, change has a knack for shaking things up when we least expect it.

But here's the deal: change isn't our adversary; it's our sparring partner in the exhilarating dance of life. Instead of dodging it like a cat avoiding a bath, why not grab change by the hand and tango together? By embracing change with open arms, we can transform what might seem like chaos into a thrilling adventure of growth and opportunity.

It's crucial to grasp that change is an inevitable part of the human experience. Just as the seasons shift and the tides ebb and flow, change is woven into the very fabric of our existence. Our lives are dynamic and ever-evolving, shaped by the choices we make and the circumstances we encounter along the way.

Acceptance plays a pivotal role in our relationship with change. Rather than resisting or fearing it, acceptance invites us to acknowledge change as a natural and necessary aspect of life. It doesn't mean we have to love every twist and turn that comes our way, but rather to recognise that fighting against change only leads to unnecessary struggle and suffering.

Once we come to terms with the inevitability of change, we can shift our perspective and embrace it as an opportunity for growth and self-discovery. Each change, whether big or small, presents us with a chance to learn, evolve, and expand our horizons.

Embracing change requires a willingness to let go of our attachment to how things "should" be and instead embrace the reality of how they are. It's about adapting to new circumstances, exploring different possibilities, and finding strength and resilience in the face of uncertainty.

1. The Change-o-Meter:
First things first, let's whip out our trusty Change-o-Meters—a nifty gadget to gauge our reactions to life's twists and turns.

Take a moment to ponder recent changes in your life, whether they're big or small. How did you initially respond to these changes? Did you greet them with a high-five or a face-palm? Rate your reaction on a scale from 1 to 10, with 1 being "I welcomed change with open arms" and 10 being "I fought change like a cat fights a bath." Then, contemplate how you can shift your mindset towards acceptance and embrace change as an opportunity for growth and self-discovery.

2. The Change Journal:

Next up, let's crack open our Change Journals—a sacred space to document our journey through life's ever-shifting landscape.

Grab a notebook or fire up your computer, and start jotting down your thoughts about recent changes in your life. Explore the rollercoaster of emotions these changes have stirred up, from excitement to apprehension and everything in between. Consider how practicing acceptance can help you ride the waves of change with grace and resilience, turning challenges into opportunities for growth and self-discovery.

3. The Change Affirmation:

Last but certainly not least, let's craft our very own Change Affirmation—a powerful mantra to remind us of the beauty and potential in embracing change.

Choose a positive affirmation that resonates with you and reflects your readiness to welcome change with open arms. For example, "I am resilient and adaptable, and I embrace change as an opportunity for growth and self-discovery." Repeat this affirmation daily, whether silently or aloud, as a beacon of strength and courage in the face of life's inevitable changes. Let these words infuse your mindset with positivity and resilience, empowering you to navigate the twists and turns of life with confidence and grace.

Journal Prompts:

1. Reflect on a recent change in your life that initially felt daunting or overwhelming. How did you react to this change, and what emotions did it stir up? Consider how acceptance could have shifted your perspective and helped you navigate this change more smoothly.

2. Explore your beliefs about change and how they influence your mindset and behaviour. Are you more inclined to embrace change with open arms, or do you tend to resist it? Contemplate how you can cultivate a mindset of acceptance and resilience in the face of life's changes.

3. Envision a future version of yourself who embraces change with acceptance and courage. What qualities does this version of you embody, and how can you cultivate these qualities in your life right now? Reflect on small steps you can take to embrace change more fully and step into your highest potential.

As we journey through life, change will inevitably be our constant companion. By cultivating a mindset of acceptance and embracing change as an opportunity for growth, we can transform the challenges we encounter into stepping stones on the path to self-discovery and fulfilment. So, let's embrace the adventure, my friends, and dance with change as our fearless partner in the beautiful symphony of life.

Celebrating Uniqueness: Loving the Quirks That Make You, You

Society loves to slap labels on us, right? They're like these neat little boxes with fancy names like "beauty queen," "brainiac," "jock," or "rebel." And sure, they might seem convenient at first glance – like a roadmap for navigating the complex landscape of human identity. Trying to squeeze yourself into one of those boxes is like trying to force a square peg into a round hole. It just doesn't fit. And let me tell you, it's not a pretty sight.

You see, when we try to conform to these narrow stereotypes, we're denying ourselves the opportunity to fully express who we are. We're hiding our quirks, our flaws, and our downright weirdness in an effort to fit in and play by society's rules. But here's the thing – when we suppress our true selves, we're not just denying ourselves the chance to shine – we're also depriving the world of our unique gifts and perspectives.

Now, let's flip the script for a moment. Imagine what happens when we fully embrace our uniqueness – when we own our quirks, our flaws, and our downright weirdness with pride and confidence. Suddenly, we're not just another face in the crowd – we're a radiant beacon of fabulousness in a sea of mediocrity. We're breaking free from the constraints of societal expectations and celebrating the beautiful messiness of being human.

Embracing our uniqueness isn't just about standing out or being different for the sake of it. It's about honouring our true selves and living authentically, without apology or shame. It's about recognising that our quirks and imperfections are what make us interesting, lovable, and undeniably human.

So, how do we get to that place of self-acceptance and celebration? Well, my friends, it all begins with acceptance – surprise, surprise, acceptance strikes again! But here's the thing about acceptance: it's not about resigning ourselves to who we are or settling for less than we deserve. It's about acknowledging and embracing all the wonderfully weird things that make us unique, and loving ourselves unconditionally, quirks and all.

Now, let's get down to business with some practical exercises to help you fully embrace your uniqueness and learn to love the quirks that make you shine:

1. The Mirror Pep Talk:
Take a moment to stand in front of the mirror and really look at yourself – quirks, flaws, and all. Instead of focusing on what you wish you could change, try dishing out some compliments like you're Oprah giving away free cars. Celebrate your quirks, your strengths, and everything that makes you uniquely you. It might feel a little silly at first, but trust me – it's a game-changer.

2. The Quirky Quest:
Think of this as a treasure hunt for your quirkiest quirks. Make a list of all the things that make you unique – from your weird hobbies to your unusual talents to your offbeat sense of humour. Then, challenge yourself to embrace and celebrate those quirks in new and exciting ways. Whether it's wearing a funky outfit, starting a quirky hobby, or sharing your weird sense of humour with the world, the key is to own it and flaunt it like the fabulous unicorn you are.

3. The Weirdness Workshop:
Time to roll up your sleeves and get down to business with some serious weirdness. Challenge yourself to do something completely out of the ordinary – whether it's trying a bizarre new food, striking up a conversation with a stranger, or taking a spontaneous adventure to a quirky local attraction. The goal here is to step outside your comfort zone, embrace the unknown, and celebrate your unique brand of weirdness.

4. The Gratitude Game:
Take a moment each day to reflect on all the things you love about yourself – quirks and all. Grab a journal and jot down three things you're grateful for about yourself. Whether it's your quirky sense of style, your eccentric taste in music, or your knack for making people laugh, celebrate the things that make you uniquely you.

Journal Prompts:

1. Reflect on your current relationship with self-acceptance and self-love. How do you perceive your quirks, flaws, and unique qualities? Are there any aspects of yourself that you struggle to embrace or accept? How can you cultivate a greater sense of self-acceptance and appreciation for your quirks?

2. Consider the ways in which your quirks and unique qualities contribute to your identity and sense of self. How do these quirks shape your interactions with others, your interests, and your passions? Are there any experiences or memories that stand out as defining moments in your journey of self-discovery and self-acceptance?

3. Explore any fears or insecurities that may be holding you back from fully embracing your uniqueness. What limiting beliefs or negative self-talk patterns are undermining your confidence and self-worth? How can you challenge these beliefs and cultivate a mindset of self-compassion and acceptance?

4. Envision your ideal vision of self-celebration and self-love. What does it look like, feel like, and sound like to fully embrace your quirks and celebrate your uniqueness? What activities, practices, or rituals would characterise this journey of self-discovery and self-acceptance? How can you take concrete steps towards realising this vision in your own life while embracing acceptance and change?

Take your time to reflect on these prompts and jot down your thoughts in your journal. Remember, self-discovery is a journey, and every step you take towards embracing your uniqueness brings you closer to living authentically and unapologetically as your true self.

Cherishing the Gift of Well-being

Now, I know what you're thinking – "gratitude" sounds all warm and fuzzy, like something you'd see embroidered on a throw pillow or hear in a yoga class. But trust me, there's more to it than just rainbows and butterflies. Gratitude is like the secret sauce of life – it adds flavour, depth, and a whole lot of goodness to our everyday experiences.

Today, we're diving deep into the world of gratitude for health – because let's face it health is wealth. And I'm not just talking about the absence of illness or disease – I'm talking about that feeling of vitality, energy, and well-being that makes you want to do a happy dance every time you wake up in the morning.

In today's fast-paced world, it's easy to take our health for granted. We get so caught up in the hustle and bustle of everyday life that we forget to pause, take a deep breath, and appreciate the incredible gift of well-being that we've been given.

Our health is like that friend who always shows up when you least expect it. It's always there, quietly supporting us in the background, until one day, it's not. And that's when we realise just how precious and fragile it really is.

Acceptance is the key to unlocking the door to gratitude and embracing the full spectrum of our health – the good, the bad, and the slightly awkward.

1. The Body Love Letter:
Get ready to shower your body with some well-deserved love and appreciation. Write yourself a love letter from head to toe, thanking each and every part of your body for all the amazing things it does for you every day. From your strong legs that carry you through life's adventures to your beating heart that keeps you alive and kicking – celebrate your body, quirks and all.

2. The Healthy Habit Tracker:
Grab a journal or a planner and create a simple tracker to monitor your health habits. This could include things like getting enough sleep, eating nourishing foods, staying hydrated, moving your body regularly, and practicing self-care. Each day, take a few minutes to check off the habits you've completed and reflect on how they contribute to your overall well-being. Not only will this help you stay accountable to your health goals, but it will also foster a sense of gratitude for the opportunity to care for your body and mind.

3. The Healthy Recipe Challenge:
Get creative in the kitchen and challenge yourself to cook up some delicious and nutritious meals. Experiment with new ingredients, flavours, and cooking techniques to nourish your body and tantalise your taste buds. As you savour each bite, take a moment to express gratitude for the abundance of fresh, wholesome food that fuels your body and supports your health.

4. The Self-Care Spa Day:
Treat yourself to a luxurious self-care spa day at home, complete with soothing baths, indulgent skincare treatments, and relaxing massages. As you pamper yourself from head to toe, express gratitude for the opportunity to prioritise your well-being and practice self-love and self-care. Remember, taking care of

yourself isn't selfish – it's essential for maintaining your health and happiness.

Journal Prompts:

1. Reflect on your current relationship with gratitude for your health. How do you perceive your body and overall well-being? Are there any aspects of your health that you tend to take for granted or overlook? How can you cultivate a greater sense of gratitude and appreciation for your body and all that it does for you?

2. Consider the ways in which your health impacts your daily life and activities. How does feeling healthy and vibrant contribute to your overall sense of happiness and fulfilment? Are there any habits or practices that you can adopt to support your health and well-being on a regular basis?

3. Explore any challenges or obstacles that you may face in maintaining gratitude for your health. What negative thought patterns or beliefs about your body and health may be holding you back from fully embracing gratitude? How can you challenge these beliefs and cultivate a mindset of acceptance and appreciation for your body and well-being?

4. Envision your ideal vision of health and well-being. What does it look like, feel like, and sound like to live a life filled with vitality, energy, and joy? What actions, habits, or practices can you incorporate into your daily routine to support your health and well-being while cultivating gratitude and acceptance for your body?

Take some time to reflect on these prompts and jot down your thoughts and feelings in your journal. Remember, gratitude for your health is a practice – and the more you cultivate it, the more you'll cherish the incredible gift of well-being that you've been given.

Rediscovering What Truly Matters

You ever find yourself buried under a mountain of stuff, wondering how in the world you accumulated so much junk? Yeah, me too. It's like my closet is in a constant state of rebellion, spitting out clothes I forgot I even owned every time I crack open the door.

Material possessions might give us a fleeting sense of happiness, but they sure as heck don't fill the void in our souls. Trust me, I've tried. I've impulse-bought enough random gadgets and gizmos to stock a small convenience store, only to realise that none of it brought me the fulfilment I craved.

So, in this chapter, we're going to Marie Kondo our lives and declutter not just our physical spaces, but our minds and hearts too. It's time to strip away the excess and rediscover what truly matters.

Set aside a weekend (or a few if you're a certified hoarder like me) and dive into the chaos. Sort through your belongings with ruthless efficiency. If it doesn't spark joy or serve a practical purpose, it's gotta go. Donate, sell, or recycle anything that's just taking up space and collecting dust.

Now, onto the mental clutter. We're talking about those toxic thoughts and negative beliefs that weigh us down. It's time for a mental spring cleaning, my friends. Start by identifying those self-limiting beliefs that are holding you back. Maybe you've convinced yourself that you're not worthy of success or that you'll never be good enough. Well, guess what? Those beliefs are straight-up garbage, and it's time to toss 'em out.

Replace those negative thoughts with affirmations of self-love and acceptance. Remind yourself that you are worthy, you are capable, and you deserve to live a life filled with joy and fulfilment. It might feel cheesy at first, but trust me, positive self-talk is like mental sunshine – it nourishes your soul and helps you grow.

Let's talk about the heart clutter – those toxic relationships and draining commitments that zap our energy and leave us feeling depleted. Surround yourself with people who lift you up, inspire you, and bring out the best in you. And don't be afraid to cut ties with those who bring nothing but drama and negativity into your life. Ain't nobody got time for that.

Once you've decluttered your life – physically, mentally, and emotionally – you'll find that you have more space to focus on what truly matters.

Take a moment to reflect on what brings you true happiness and fulfilment. Maybe it's spending quality time with loved ones, pursuing your passions, or making a difference in the world. Whatever it is, make it a priority in your life. Invest your time, energy, and resources into the things that light you up and bring you joy.

True happiness doesn't come from what you have, but from who you are and how you choose to live your life. So let go of the need to keep up with the Joneses and embrace a simpler, more meaningful way of living.

Now, I'm not saying you have to swear off material possessions altogether. I mean, I still love me some cute shoes and fancy gadgets. But let's shift our focus from acquiring stuff to creating experiences. Invest in memories, not things. Spend your money on travel, adventures, and meaningful experiences that enrich your life and feed your soul.

So here's your homework for this chapter:

1. Declutter Your Physical Space:
Start by dedicating a specific time slot in your schedule for decluttering your physical environment. This could be a weekend afternoon or even just an hour each day throughout the week. The key is to commit to this time and make it a priority.

Begin by focusing on one area of your home at a time. Whether it's your closet, kitchen, or workspace, tackle one space before moving on to the next. This will help prevent overwhelm and ensure that you give each area the attention it deserves.

As you go through your belongings, ask yourself a simple question: Does this item bring me joy or serve a practical purpose in my life? If the answer is no, it's time to let it go. Set aside items to donate, sell, or recycle, and be ruthless in your decision-making process.

To make the decluttering process more manageable, break it down into smaller tasks. For example, focus on decluttering one shelf or drawer at a time rather than trying to tackle an entire room in one go. Celebrate your progress along the way, and don't be afraid to ask for help if you need it.

2. Declutter Your Mind:
Decluttering your mind involves identifying and challenging those self-limiting beliefs that are holding you back from living your best life. Start by setting aside some quiet time for introspection and self-reflection.

Grab a journal or notebook and write down any negative thoughts or beliefs that come to mind. These could be things like "I'm not good enough" or "I'll never succeed." Once you've identified these beliefs, challenge them with evidence to the contrary.

For example, if you believe you're not good enough, write down all the times you've succeeded or received positive feedback from others. Use these examples to create positive affirmations that counteract your negative beliefs.

Practice repeating these affirmations daily, especially when you notice negative thoughts creeping in. Over time, you'll rewire your brain to focus on the positive and cultivate a mindset of self-love and acceptance.

3. Declutter Your Heart:

Evaluate your relationships and commitments with honesty and compassion. Take stock of the people and activities in your life that energise you and bring you joy, as well as those that drain your energy and leave you feeling depleted.

Identify any toxic relationships or commitments that no longer serve your highest good. This could include friendships that are one-sided or draining, or obligations that you've taken on out of guilt or obligation.

Once you've identified these toxic elements, make a plan to let them go. This might involve setting boundaries with certain individuals, ending unhealthy relationships, or stepping back from commitments that no longer align with your values and priorities.

As you release these toxic connections, make room for positive, uplifting influences in your life. Surround yourself with people who support and encourage you, and prioritise activities that bring you joy and fulfilment.

4. Reflect on What Truly Matters:

Take some time to reflect on what truly brings you happiness and fulfilment in life. This could be spending time with loved ones, pursuing your passions, or making a positive impact in your community.

Grab your journal and make a list of the things that bring you joy and fulfilment. Consider how you can prioritise these things in your life and make time for them on a regular basis.

As you reflect on what truly matters, think about how you can align your daily actions and decisions with your values and priorities. This might involve saying no to things that don't align with your goals, and saying yes to opportunities that bring you closer to your dreams.

Journal Prompts:

1. What physical possessions can I declutter to create more space and clarity in my life?

2. What self-limiting beliefs am I holding onto, and how can I replace them with affirmations of self-love and acceptance?

3. Which relationships and commitments in my life are draining my energy, and how can I create healthier boundaries?

4. What experiences bring me the greatest joy and fulfilment, and how can I prioritise them in my life?

Remember, decluttering your life is an ongoing process, and it's okay to start small. Celebrate your progress along the way, and be gentle with yourself as you navigate this journey of self-discovery and growth.

It's not about how much you have, but how deeply you appreciate what you do have. So let's declutter our lives and make room for what truly matters. You got this!

The Power of Silence: Finding Solace in Quiet Reflection

Prepare to have your mind blown because silence is so much more than just a lack of sound. It's a powerful tool for finding peace, clarity, and inner strength.

So, picture this: you're sitting in a room, surrounded by nothing but silence. No buzzing phones, no chatty coworkers, just you and your thoughts. Sounds terrifying, right? Well, buckle up, because we're diving headfirst into the wonderful world of silence.

Silence is awkward, uncomfortable, and downright terrifying for some people. But silence is where the magic happens. It's where we can finally hear ourselves think, tune into our inner voice, and find solace in the chaos of everyday life.

Let's be real – embracing silence is easier said than done. In a world filled with constant noise and distractions, finding moments of quiet reflection can feel like a Herculean

First things first, let's address the elephant in the room – the fear of silence. We live in a society that glorifies busyness and equates silence with laziness or boredom. But here's the tea: silence is not the enemy, it's our greatest ally in the quest for inner peace and self-discovery.

So, how do we learn to embrace the silence without spiralling into a pit of existential dread? Well, it all starts with setting aside dedicated time for quiet reflection. Carve out a few minutes each day to disconnect from the outside world and tune into your inner thoughts and feelings.

Now, I know what you're thinking – "But Emily, I don't have time for silence! I've got a million things on my to-do list!" Trust me, I get it. But here's the thing: if you don't make time for silence, you'll never truly know yourself or what you're capable of.

So, let's get practical. Here are a few exercises to help you embrace the power of silence and find solace in quiet reflection:

1. The Silence Challenge:
For this exercise, I challenge you to carve out just five minutes of silence each day. Find a quiet space where you won't be disturbed, set a timer, and simply sit in silence. Notice any thoughts or emotions that arise, but resist the urge to engage with them. Instead, allow yourself to simply be present in the moment. If your mind starts to wander (and trust me, it will), gently bring your focus back to your breath. The goal here isn't to clear your mind completely – it's to cultivate a sense of presence and awareness in the present moment.
Trust me, even just five minutes of silence can work wonders for your mental well-being.

The power of solitude. In our hyper-connected world, we're constantly surrounded by other people – whether it's in-person interactions or virtual connections through social media. But solitude offers us a precious opportunity to unplug, recharge, and reconnect with ourselves.

2. Solo Date Night:
For this exercise, treat yourself to a solo date night. Choose an activity that you enjoy – whether it's going for a walk in nature, treating yourself to a fancy dinner, or curling up with a good book. The key is to do it alone, without the distractions of other people. Use this time to reflect on your thoughts and feelings, and enjoy the freedom of your own company.

The art of mindful listening. In our noisy world, we're often so focused on talking that we forget to truly listen. But in silence, we have the opportunity to become better listeners.

3. The Soundscape Meditation:
Find a comfortable space where you won't be disturbed, and sit or lie down in a relaxed position. Close your eyes and take a few deep breaths to centre yourself.

Now, bring your awareness to the sounds around you. Listen carefully to every noise in the room – the hum of the air conditioner, the rustling of leaves outside, the distant chatter of voices. Pay attention to each sound, no matter how faint or insignificant it may seem.

As you listen, resist the urge to judge or label the sounds. Instead, approach them with an open mind and a sense of curiosity. Notice how each sound comes and goes, rising and falling like waves in the ocean.

If your mind starts to wander or you become distracted, gently bring your focus back to the sounds around you. Allow yourself to be fully present in the moment, immersed in the symphony of noises that surround you.

Continue this practice for a few minutes, or as long as you feel comfortable. When you're ready, slowly open your eyes and take a moment to reflect on your experience.

4. The Acceptance Meditation:
For this exercise, find a comfortable position and close your eyes. Take a few deep breaths and allow yourself to relax. Now, repeat the following affirmation silently to yourself: "I accept myself exactly as I am." Allow yourself to fully embody this affirmation, embracing all aspects of yourself – the good, the bad, and the messy. Notice any resistance that arises, but gently let it go and return to the affirmation. Practice this meditation regularly to cultivate a deep sense of self-acceptance and inner peace.

So there you have it, folks – the power of silence. Embrace it, cherish it, and let it guide you on your journey to inner peace and self-discovery.

Journal Prompts:
1. How do I feel when I embrace silence? What thoughts and emotions arise?

2. What activities bring me the most joy and fulfilment when I'm alone?

3. How can I become a better listener – both to others and to myself?

4. What aspects of myself am I struggling to accept, and how can I cultivate a greater sense of self-acceptance?

5. Reflect on your experience of listening to every noise in the room. What sounds stood out to you the most? How did you feel while engaging in this practice? Did you notice any changes in your perception of sound or your overall sense of well-being?

Remember, silence isn't just about the absence of noise – it's about finding solace, clarity, and acceptance within yourself. Embrace the power of silence as a tool for self-discovery and inner peace. Allow yourself to bask in the stillness, knowing that within the silence lies the strength to navigate life's challenges with grace and resilience. So take a moment to savour the silence, and let it guide you on your journey to acceptance and fulfilment.

Acceptance in Uncertain Times: Navigating the Unknown with Grace

Well, well, well, here we are, navigating through the murky waters of uncertainty like a bunch of sailors without a compass. But fear not, because in this chapter, we're going to sprinkle a little acceptance magic on this chaotic situation and come out the other side with our sanity intact...hopefully.

Before we delve any further, it's imperative that we confront the obvious issue at hand: uncertainty sucks. It's like trying to drive through dense fog with your headlights off. You have no idea what's ahead, and every bump in the road feels like a potential disaster waiting to happen. But instead of white-knuckling it through this fog of uncertainty, how about we embrace it with open arms? Crazy, right? Hear me out.

Acceptance doesn't mean we roll over and let uncertainty steamroll us. No, no, no. Acceptance means acknowledging that, hey, life is unpredictable, and sometimes things don't go according to plan. And you know what? That's okay. It's like going to a restaurant and ordering your favourite dish, only to find out they're out of it. Are you going to throw a tantrum and demand they conjure it up out of thin air? Probably not (though, let's be honest, the thought might cross your mind). Instead, you accept the situation, peruse the menu again, and maybe discover a new favourite.

So, how do we apply this acceptance mojo to our lives, especially when the world feels like it's spinning off its axis? Well, grab your pens and get ready to jot down some practical exercises.

1. The Serenity Prayer Shuffle:
You've probably heard the Serenity Prayer a gazillion times, but have you ever really let it sink in? It goes a little something like this: "Grant me the serenity to accept the things I cannot change, the courage to change the things I can, and the wisdom to know the difference." So, let's put it into action.

Grab a piece of paper and divide it into three columns. In the first column, jot down all the things in your life that you can't control. Go ahead, let it all out. From traffic jams to global pandemics, write it down.

In the second column, list the things you can control. Maybe it's your daily routine, your attitude, or how many episodes of that new Netflix series you binge-watch tonight.

Now, here's the kicker. In the third column, write down the things you're not sure about. These are the grey areas, the wildcards, the curveballs life throws your way. Instead of stressing over them, acknowledge their existence and let them be.

2. The "Leap of Faith" Trust Fall:
Ah, the trust fall. It's the ultimate test of, well, trust. But instead of falling backward into the waiting arms of a friend, how about we take a leap of faith into the great unknown?

Find a quiet spot where you can be alone with your thoughts (and maybe a fluffy pillow for good measure). Close your eyes, take a deep breath, and visualise yourself standing at the edge of a cliff.

Feel the wind on your face and the butterflies in your stomach as you prepare to take the plunge.

Now, here's the fun part. Instead of picturing a rocky demise at the bottom of the cliff, imagine yourself soaring through the air like a majestic eagle. Feel the exhilaration of letting go and trusting that everything will work out in the end.

3. The "What's the Worst That Could Happen?" Game:
Okay, I know what you're thinking. "But Emily, I already play this game every time I have to make a decision." Ah, but do you play it with a twist?

Instead of fixating on the worst-case scenario like it's your job, let's flip the script. Take a deep breath and ask yourself, "What's the worst that could happen...and then what?" Keep going until you reach the absolute worst-case scenario. Chances are, it's not as catastrophic as your anxious mind would have you believe.

Once you've reached rock bottom, take a step back and look at the big picture. Suddenly, that looming cloud of uncertainty doesn't seem so menacing, does it?

Journal Prompts:

1. How do you typically respond to uncertainty? Do you tend to fight it, flee from it, or freeze in its tracks?

2. Think of a recent situation where uncertainty reared its ugly head. How did you handle it? What could you have done differently?

3. Imagine yourself floating down a river of uncertainty. What would it feel like to surrender to the current and let it carry you where it may?

4. What's one small step you can take today to embrace uncertainty and invite acceptance into your life?

5. Bonus round: Write a letter to your future self, reflecting on how you've grown through navigating uncertainty with grace and acceptance.

Acceptance isn't about waving a white flag and surrendering to the chaos. It's about finding the beauty in the unknown, embracing the adventure, and trusting in the journey, even when the path ahead is shrouded in fog. So, let's raise a toast to uncertainty—to the unexpected twists, the hidden treasures, and the lessons learned along the way. Here's to navigating the unknown with grace, courage, and a whole lot of acceptance.

Respecting Your Energy: Setting Boundaries for Sustainable Vitality

Energy—the elusive yet essential essence that fuels our every action and breath. It's like a delicate flower, easily withered if not tended to with care. In the tumultuous whirlwind of life, our energy becomes the currency we trade, often giving more than we can afford. We find ourselves stretched thin, pulled in every direction by the demands of work, relationships, and the world at large.

We're not powerless victims of circumstance. No, we are warriors, equipped with the mighty power of boundaries. Picture it: not swords in hand, but firm lines drawn in the sand, marking the limits of what we will allow to drain our precious energy.

In this chapter, we're not just learning about boundaries; we're mastering the art of energy preservation. It's about recognising that our time and vitality are finite resources, worthy of protection and respect. So, grab your metaphorical swords—your pens, your voices, your unwavering resolve—and let's embark on this journey together.

We're not just slaying energy vampires; we're reclaiming our autonomy and agency in a world that often demands too much. With each boundary set, we reclaim a piece of ourselves, cultivating a sense of inner peace and balance amidst the chaos.

So, join me as we arm ourselves with boundaries and venture forth into the battlefield of life. Together, we'll forge a path toward sustainable vitality, honouring our energy and reclaiming our power one boundary at a time.

1. The "Hell Yes or Hell No" Declaration:
Alrighty, time to channel your inner superhero and declare your boundaries like a boss. Picture yourself donning a cape and soaring through the sky, because you're about to become the master of your own energy destiny.

Grab a piece of paper and draw a line down the middle to create two columns. In the first column, list down all the activities, commitments, and people in your life that make you feel like you could conquer the world. These are your "hell yes" moments—embrace them like the rockstar you are.

In the second column, jot down the things that drain your energy faster than a kid guzzling a juice box. Maybe it's that friend who always leaves you feeling like you've run a marathon, or that soul-sucking job that's slowly draining the life out of you. These are your "hell no" triggers—time to bid them adieu.

Now, let's get down to business. Take a good, hard look at your list and ask yourself: How can I say "hell yes" to more of the good stuff and "hell no" to the energy vampires? It's time to start prioritising your precious energy like the VIP guest it is.

2. The "No" Muscle Flex:
Think of it as a workout for your soul, except instead of dumbbells, you're lifting the weight of unnecessary obligations and guilt trips.

Find a mirror (preferably one that makes you look like a total badass) and strike a power pose. Stand tall, shoulders back, and repeat after me: "Nope, not today!"

Let's put this newfound confidence into practice. Think of a recent request or commitment that made you want to crawl under a rock and hibernate until the end of time. Maybe it was agreeing to organise your cousin's third baby shower this year, or attending yet another virtual meeting that could've been an email. Sound familiar?

Take a deep breath, channel your inner warrior, and say it with me: "No, thank you." That's it, you did it! Flex that "no" muscle like the boss you are and revel in the newfound freedom that comes with setting boundaries like a pro.

3. The Energy Audit Extravaganza:
It's time to put on your detective hat and go full Sherlock Holmes on your energy reserves. Grab your magnifying glass (or, you know, just your trusty notebook) and let's get sleuthing.

Start by jotting down a typical day in the life of [insert your fabulous name here]. From the moment you drag yourself out of bed to the second you collapse onto the couch in a heap of exhaustion, leave no detail untouched.

Now, it's time to play detective. Take a good, hard look at your energy investments throughout the day. Are you spending too much time on activities that drain your energy faster than a leaky faucet? Maybe it's that soul-sucking job or that friend who always seems to suck the life out of you like a vampire. Or perhaps you're neglecting those little moments of joy and self-care that fuel your soul and recharge your batteries.

Once you've identified your energy drains and gains, it's time to make some tough decisions. What can you delegate, eliminate, or renegotiate to create more space for the things that light you up like a Christmas tree? Remember, you're the CEO of your own energy empire—time to start calling the shots like a boss.

Journal Prompts:

1. Reflect on a time when you said "yes" to something that drained your energy. How did it make you feel? What could you have done differently to protect your energy?

2. Imagine your ideal day—a day filled with activities that energise and inspire you. What does it look like? How can you start incorporating more of these moments into your life?

3. Think of a recent situation where you felt guilty for saying "no" to a request or commitment. Why did you feel guilty? How can you reframe your mindset around setting boundaries?

4. Visualise yourself as a fierce boundary-setting warrior, standing tall and confident in your ability to protect your precious energy. How does it feel to take control of your energy like a boss?

5. Bonus round: Write a letter to your future self, celebrating all the progress you've made in setting boundaries and respecting your energy. How has it transformed your life for the better?

As we wrap up this exhilarating journey through the realm of boundary-setting and energy preservation, remember this: respecting your energy is not just an act of self-care, but a revolutionary act of self-love. By setting boundaries and prioritising your well-being, you're not only reclaiming your power but also paving the way for a life filled with sustainable vitality and joy.

The Joy of Giving: Cultivating a Generous Heart

So, we've talked about setting boundaries and protecting our precious energy like it's the last piece of chocolate in a room full of hungry toddlers. But now, let's switch gears and dive into the delightful world of giving. That's right, we're talking about spreading joy, sharing love, and flexing those generosity muscles like they're going out of style.

Now, I know what you're thinking: "I'm already stretched thin like a pair of cheap leggings on Black Friday."

Giving isn't just about doling out cash or sacrificing your sanity—it's about cultivating a generous heart and finding joy in the act of giving, no matter how big or small.

So, grab your superhero capes (because let's face it, giving makes you feel like a freaking superhero) and let's spread some love like confetti at a wedding.

1. The Random Acts of Kindness Extravaganza:
Who doesn't love a good ol' fashioned kindness parade? Picture it: you, marching down the street, tossing out smiles and compliments like they're candy at a parade. Sounds pretty awesome, right? Well, get ready to unleash your inner kindness warrior, because we're about to spread some serious joy.

Start by brainstorming a list of random acts of kindness you can perform throughout the day. It could be as simple as holding the door open for a stranger, paying for someone's coffee in line behind you, or leaving a sweet note for a coworker.

Now, here's the fun part: pick a day (or heck, make it every day) and challenge yourself to complete as many acts of kindness as possible. Keep track of your deeds in a journal and revel in the warm fuzzies that come from knowing you've made someone's day just a little bit brighter.

2. The "Give What You Can" Game Show:
Who says giving has to break the bank? Not me, that's for sure! In this game show extravaganza, we're throwing out the rulebook and embracing the joy of giving, no matter how big or small.

Grab a friend (or fly solo if you're feeling adventurous) and embark on a mission to spread joy without spending a dime. Maybe it's volunteering at a local soup kitchen, donating clothes to a homeless shelter, or simply offering a listening ear to someone in need. The possibilities are endless—get creative and let your generosity shine like a beacon of hope in a world that could always use a little more love.

As you embark on your giving adventure, remember this: it's not about the size of the gift, but the intention behind it. Whether you're giving your time, your talents, or your treasure, know that every act of kindness has the power to make a difference in someone's life.

3. The Gratitude Attitude Adjustment:
Ah, gratitude—the secret sauce that makes life taste a little sweeter. In this exercise, we're not just giving; we're cultivating an attitude of gratitude that will transform the way we see the world.

Start by taking a moment to reflect on all the blessings in your life, big and small. Maybe it's the roof over your head, the food on your table, or the people who love you unconditionally. Whatever it is, take a moment to bask in the warm glow of gratitude and let it fill your heart like a cozy blanket on a cold winter's day.

Instead of just counting your blessings, why not pay it forward? Make a list of all the things you're grateful for and brainstorm ways you can give back to others who may not be as fortunate. Maybe it's donating to a local charity, volunteering at a community centre, or simply spreading kindness wherever you go. The choice is yours—let your gratitude guide you as you embark on this giving journey.

Journal Prompts:

1. Reflect on a time when someone's act of kindness made your day. How did it make you feel? What impact did it have on your outlook on life?

2. Think of a recent situation where you had the opportunity to give back to someone in need. How did it feel to make a difference in their life? What did you learn from the experience?

3. Imagine a world where everyone embraced the joy of giving. What would it look like? How can you contribute to creating a more generous and compassionate society?

4. Consider the people in your life who have supported you, loved you, and lifted you up during challenging times. How can you show your appreciation and gratitude for their kindness?

5. Bonus round: Write a letter to your future self, reflecting on the impact of cultivating a generous heart and embracing the joy of giving. How has it enriched your life and the lives of those around you?

Generosity isn't just about giving material possessions—it's about spreading love, kindness, and compassion wherever you go. By cultivating a generous heart and embracing the joy of giving, we not only make the world a brighter place for others but also experience a profound sense of fulfilment and connection within ourselves. So, let's continue to shower the world with our boundless love and generosity, knowing that even the smallest acts of kindness can make a world of difference.

Letting Go of Perfectionism: Embracing the Beauty in Mistakes

Now, I'll be the first to admit that this is a tough one for me. As a recovering perfectionist myself, I know all too well the pressure we put on ourselves to get everything just right.
Perfectionism is a sneaky little monster that robs us of joy, drains our energy, and leaves us feeling like we're constantly falling short.

So, how do we break free from the perfectionism trap? Well, it starts with a little thing called acceptance. We need to accept that we're human, which means we're messy, flawed, and oh-so-perfectly imperfect. And you know what? That's okay. More than okay, actually. It's downright liberating.

One of the best ways to practice letting go of perfectionism is by embracing the beauty in our mistakes. Instead of beating ourselves up every time we mess up, let's celebrate those moments as opportunities for growth and learning. After all, some of the greatest discoveries and innovations in history have come from happy accidents and epic failures.

1. Make a "Messy Wins" List:
Grab a pen and paper (or your favourite note-taking app) and start jotting down all the times when things didn't go according to plan but turned out surprisingly well in the end. Maybe you spilled coffee on your shirt right before a big presentation, but your impromptu joke about being a walking coffee advertisement actually got the whole room laughing and relaxed. Whatever it is, celebrate those messy wins and remind yourself that perfection is overrated.

2. Try Something New (and Mess It Up on Purpose):
This one might sound a little counterintuitive, but bear with me. Pick something you've always wanted to try but have been too afraid to because you're worried about messing up. Maybe it's painting, cooking a fancy recipe, or even singing karaoke. Whatever it is, give yourself permission to be absolutely terrible at it. Embrace the mistakes, laugh them off, and revel in the joy of trying something new without the pressure to be perfect.

3. Create a "Fail Forward" Mantra:
Whenever you catch yourself slipping back into perfectionist mode, repeat this mantra to yourself: "I embrace imperfection, and I grow from my mistakes." Remind yourself that failure is not the end of the world; it's simply a stepping stone on the path to success. By reframing failure as an essential part of the learning process, you'll start to see mistakes not as roadblocks but as opportunities to become stronger, wiser, and more resilient.

Journal Prompts:

1. Reflect on a specific situation where your pursuit of perfectionism has hindered your progress or caused unnecessary stress. Describe the scenario in detail, including how you felt and how your perfectionist tendencies influenced your actions. Consider how this experience has impacted your overall well-being and sense of self-worth.

2. Explore the origins of your perfectionist tendencies. Think back to your childhood and upbringing, and consider any experiences or messages from family members, teachers, or peers that may have contributed to your perfectionistic mindset. How have these early influences shaped your beliefs about success, failure, and self-worth?

3. Imagine a future version of yourself who has fully embraced imperfection and let go of the need to be perfect. What does this version of yourself look like? How does it feel to live without the constant pressure to measure up to impossible standards? Envision the ways in which this shift in mindset would positively impact your relationships, career, and overall quality of life.

4. Identify three specific areas of your life where perfectionism tends to show up most frequently (e.g., work, relationships, personal goals). For each area, brainstorm alternative ways of thinking and behaving that align with the principles of acceptance and self-compassion. How can you cultivate a more balanced and realistic approach to success and achievement in these areas?

5. Consider the role of self-compassion in overcoming perfectionism. Reflect on times when you have shown kindness and understanding toward yourself in the face of failure or disappointment. How did practicing self-

compassion affect your ability to bounce back from setbacks and move forward with resilience? What strategies can you implement to cultivate a greater sense of self-compassion in your daily life?

6. Think about the people in your life who embody the qualities of authenticity, vulnerability, and acceptance. What can you learn from their example? How can you surround yourself with individuals who support and encourage you to embrace imperfection and live authentically?

7. Imagine writing a letter to your inner perfectionist. What would you say to this part of yourself? How would you express gratitude for its efforts to protect you while also gently encouraging it to loosen its grip and make room for growth and self-discovery?

8. Take a moment to celebrate your progress on the journey toward embracing imperfection. Reflect on moments when you have challenged yourself to step outside of your comfort zone, take risks, and embrace the unknown. How have these experiences contributed to your personal growth and resilience? What insights have you gained about yourself along the way?

9. Consider the concept of "failing forward" as a valuable tool for learning and growth. Think about a recent setback or failure that you have experienced and reflect on the lessons you have learned from the experience. How can you use this newfound wisdom to approach similar challenges in the future with greater courage and resilience?

10. Visualise a future version of yourself who has fully embraced imperfection and lives with a deep sense of acceptance and self-love. What daily practices and habits can you incorporate into your life to nurture this vision and cultivate a greater sense of peace, joy, and authenticity?

Remember, my tired but tenacious friends, perfectionism is just fear in fancy clothing. It's time to strip away those layers of self-doubt and embrace the beautifully messy reality of being human. So go ahead, make mistakes, take risks, and above all, have fun along the way.

The Beauty of Diversity: Celebrating Differences in Others

I don't know about you, but I've always been a big fan of diversity. Whether it's in the form of different cultures, backgrounds, perspectives, or even just quirky personality traits, I truly believe that diversity is what makes the world go round. After all, life would be pretty darn boring if we were all exactly the same, wouldn't it?

While we may intellectually understand the importance of diversity, truly embracing and celebrating our differences can be a bit trickier. We're often taught to fear the unknown, to stick with what's familiar, and to view anything that deviates from the norm as a threat. But let me tell you, my friends, nothing could be further from the truth.

The beauty of diversity lies in its ability to expand our horizons, challenge our assumptions, and enrich our lives in ways we never could have imagined. When we open ourselves up to different perspectives and experiences, we not only gain a deeper understanding of the world around us but also foster greater empathy, compassion, and connection with others.

So how do we go about celebrating diversity in our everyday lives? Well, I'm glad you asked! Here are a few real practical exercises to help you get started:

1. Step Outside Your Comfort Zone:
One of the best ways to embrace diversity is by exposing yourself to people, cultures, and experiences that are different from your own. This could mean trying a new cuisine, attending a cultural festival, or striking up a conversation with someone who has a different background or perspective than you. Get curious, ask questions, and approach each new encounter with an open mind and heart.

2. Challenge Your Assumptions:
We all have biases and stereotypes that influence the way we see the world. Take some time to reflect on your own assumptions and preconceived notions about people who are different from you. Are there any beliefs or attitudes that you've

been holding onto without question? Challenge yourself to question the validity of these assumptions and explore alternative perspectives.

3. Practice Active Listening:
One of the most powerful ways to show respect and appreciation for someone else's perspective is by actively listening to what they have to say. Put down your phone, maintain eye contact, and give the other person your full attention. Resist the urge to interrupt or interject with your own opinions, and instead, focus on truly understanding their point of view.

4. Seek Out Diverse Media:
Expand your cultural horizons by diversifying your media consumption. Whether it's books, movies, music, or podcasts, make an effort to seek out content created by and featuring people from diverse backgrounds. Not only will this expose you to new ideas and perspectives, but it will also support creators who are often underrepresented in mainstream media.

5. Celebrate Differences in Your Community:
Take proactive steps to create a more inclusive and welcoming environment in your community. This could involve volunteering with organisations that promote diversity and inclusion, advocating for policies that support marginalised communities, or simply reaching out to neighbours and acquaintances to build connections across cultural lines.

Journal Prompts:

1. Reflect on a time when you felt uncomfortable or out of place in a diverse setting. What were the underlying beliefs or fears that contributed to your discomfort? How can you challenge these beliefs and cultivate a greater sense of openness and acceptance toward diversity in the future?

2. Think about a person in your life who embodies the values of diversity and inclusion. What qualities or actions make them stand out as a champion of diversity? How can you incorporate these values into your own life and relationships?

3. Consider the ways in which your own cultural background and experiences have shaped your perspective on diversity. How have your cultural identity and upbringing influenced the way you interact with people from different backgrounds? Are there any biases or assumptions that you need to examine more closely?

4. Imagine a future in which diversity is celebrated and embraced in every aspect of society. What steps can you take personally to contribute to this vision? How can you use your voice and influence to advocate for greater inclusivity and representation in your community?

5. Reflect on a recent experience or encounter that challenged your assumptions about diversity. What did you learn from this experience? How has it influenced your attitudes and behaviours toward diversity moving forward?

Diversity is not something to be feared or avoided; it's something to be celebrated and embraced. By opening our hearts and minds to the rich tapestry of human experience, we can create a world that is more vibrant, inclusive, and compassionate for all.

Mindful Decision-Making: Choosing Paths Aligned with Your Values

Decisions – those unpredictable rollercoasters of life. One moment, we find ourselves riding high on the winds of certainty, exhilarated by the clarity of our choices. The next, we're plummeting into the abyss of indecision, spiralling downward faster than the speed of thought, trapped in the suffocating grip of what we affectionately call "analysis paralysis."

At the core of mindful decision-making lies the art of attunement – the ability to listen keenly to the whispers of our inner compass and stay anchored to the bedrock of our values, even as the tempest of choices swirls around us. By approaching decisions with a spirit of mindfulness and self-awareness, we unlock the power to discern which paths resonate most deeply with our true selves, guiding us toward fulfilment and authenticity in our pursuits.

But you may wonder, dear friends, how does one cultivate this sacred practice of mindful decision-making? Ah, fret not, for I shall impart unto you the secrets of the ancients, passed down through generations of wise sages and decision-making savants. Listen closely as I unveil a treasure trove of practical strategies and profound insights to elevate you to the esteemed rank of decision-making virtuoso.

First and foremost, let us embark on a journey of introspection, delving deep into the recesses of our souls to unearth the bedrock of our values. Take heed, my friends, for a ship without a compass is doomed to wander aimlessly upon the turbulent seas of life. Through reflection and contemplation, we shall forge a steadfast moral compass, guiding us unerringly toward decisions that align with our deepest convictions and aspirations.

Next, let us embrace the power of mindfulness – the art of being fully present in the moment, attuned to the subtle nuances of our thoughts, feelings, and desires. In the cacophony of life's distractions, mindfulness serves as our steady anchor, grounding us in the here and now, and empowering us to make decisions with clarity and purpose.

But alas, my fellow travellers, mindfulness alone is not enough to navigate the treacherous waters of decision-making. We must also cultivate the art of discernment – the ability to sift through the myriad options before us, weighing their merits against the backdrop of our values and aspirations. Through discernment, we gain the clarity and insight to distinguish between fleeting temptations and enduring truths, guiding us toward decisions that honour our deepest desires and aspirations.

And finally, let us not forget the power of action – the courage to take bold strides forward, even in the face of uncertainty and doubt. For it is in the crucible of action that our decisions are truly tested, and our destinies forged. So let us march boldly forward, my friends, armed with the wisdom of the ages and the courage of our convictions, as we embark on the grand adventure of mindful decision-making.

So there you have it, dear friends – a roadmap to mastery in the art of decision-making, forged through the fires of introspection, mindfulness, discernment, and action. May you wield these tools with wisdom and grace, guiding you unerringly toward a future rich with purpose, fulfilment, and authenticity.

1. Get Clear on Your Values:
Before you can make decisions that align with your values, you need to know what those values are. Take some time to reflect on what matters most to you in life. Is it family, honesty, creativity, adventure, or something else entirely? Make a list of your top values and prioritise them in order of importance.

2. Practice the 10-10-10 Rule:
When faced with a tough decision, use the 10-10-10 rule to gain perspective. Ask yourself: How will I feel about this decision 10 minutes from now? How about 10 months from now? And finally, how will I feel about it 10 years from now? This exercise can help you see the bigger picture and make choices that are in line with your long-term goals and values.

3. Listen to Your Gut:
Your intuition is a powerful tool when it comes to decision-making. Pay attention to how your body and mind react to different options. Do you feel a sense of ease and excitement, or do you feel tense and anxious? Trust your gut instincts and use them as a guide to steer you toward choices that feel right for you.

4. Practice Self-Compassion:
Making decisions can be stressful, especially when there's no clear right or wrong answer. Be kind to yourself throughout the decision-making process and acknowledge that it's okay to feel uncertain or conflicted. Remind yourself that you're doing the best you can with the information and resources available to you.

5. Visualise Your Ideal Outcome:

Take a moment to visualise what your life will look like once you've made a decision. Picture yourself living out the consequences of each option and pay attention to how each scenario makes you feel. Use this visualisation exercise to gain clarity and confidence in your decision-making process.

By incorporating these exercises into your decision-making toolkit, you can approach choices with greater mindfulness, confidence, and alignment with your values.

Journal Prompts:

1. Reflect on a recent decision you made that was aligned with your values. What factors influenced your decision-making process? How did it feel to make a choice that was in line with what matters most to you? What did you learn about yourself in the process?

2. Think about a time when you made a decision that went against your values. What were the consequences of this decision? How did it impact your well-being and sense of integrity? What steps can you take to prevent similar situations from arising in the future?

3. Consider a decision you're currently facing that feels particularly challenging or overwhelming. Take some time to explore the different options available to you and how each aligns with your values. What insights or clarity do you gain from this reflection? How can you use this awareness to move forward with confidence and conviction?

4. Imagine yourself as the protagonist of your own life story, faced with a pivotal decision that will shape the course of your journey. What values guide your decision-making process in this scenario? How does embracing mindfulness and self-awareness empower you to choose a path that aligns with your deepest desires and aspirations?

5. Reflect on the role of acceptance in the decision-making process. How can you cultivate a greater sense of acceptance for the outcomes of your decisions, regardless of whether they unfold as planned? How does practicing acceptance allow you to approach decision-making with greater courage, resilience, and peace of mind?

So there you have it, my tired but tenacious friends! Armed with these real practical exercises and a newfound commitment to mindfulness and self-awareness, you're ready to tackle even the trickiest of decisions with grace and gusto. Remember, trust yourself, listen to your gut, and always choose paths that align with your values. With each mindful decision you make, you're not just shaping your future, you're living a life that's true to who you are. So go ahead, embrace the beauty of mindful decision-making, and watch as your journey unfolds with clarity, purpose, and a whole lot of fabulousness!

A New Dawn—Reclaiming Your Vitality through Acceptance

Oh, my goodness, buckle up, my tired, but not lazy comrades! Can you believe we've made it to the end of this wild ride? I'm sitting here, surrounded by empty coffee cups and half-eaten snacks, feeling like I've just survived an epic battle with fatigue. But you know what? We did it, and we did it together, armed with nothing but the power of acceptance.

Acceptance, my friends, is like the ultimate weapon against the forces of exhaustion. It's like saying to the universe, "Hey, I see you, I acknowledge you, but I'm not letting you drag me down." It's like slaying dragons with a side of self-love and a sprinkle of sass.

And let me tell you, accepting your tiredness too is not a sign of weakness; it's a badge of honour. It's like wearing a "I Survived Another Day" sticker proudly on your forehead, daring anyone to challenge your resilience.

To all of you out there feeling like you're swimming upstream in a river of espresso, I want you to know something: you are powerful beyond measure. You are the captain of your own ship, steering through the choppy waters of life with nothing but sheer determination and maybe a little bit of dry shampoo.

Life is messy, my friends. It's like trying to juggle flaming torches while riding a unicycle on a tightrope. But guess what? You've got this. You've got the balance, the grace, and the fiery spirit to conquer anything that comes your way.

As we bid adieu to this chapter of our lives, let's take a moment to savour the sweet taste of victory. Let's raise our tired, but not lazy arms in triumph and shout to the heavens, "I am fierce, I am fabulous, and I am freaking exhausted!"

And hey, if you ever need a pep talk or a virtual hug, you know where to find me. Feel free to slide into my DMs, shoot me an email (emily.emma.roberts@gmail.com) or follow me on social media for all the latest updates and shenanigans.

Until we meet again, my fellow warriors of weariness, keep shining bright like the exhausted diamonds that you are. And never forget: you are tired, not lazy, and your vitality awaits on the other side of acceptance.

Printed in Great Britain
by Amazon